Successful
Foster Care
Adoption

Emotional Journey, Uncommon Love

DEBORAH A. BEASLEY

Together At Last Family Press

Praise

"As I read Deborah Beasley's essential resource *Successful Foster Care Adoption*, I continually was able to relate the topics Deborah addressed in the book to my experiences as a middle school guidance counselor. Even in ideal circumstances in which the adoptive parents are amazing people and their "new" children are resilient survivors, there are unique stressors – and parental love is not enough. These frustrations and challenges often spill over at school. *Successful Foster Care Adoption* is an essential tool not only for parents, but for guidance counselors and other child service providers at well."

"Through Deborah's experience as an adoptive parent and parent coach, she expertly presents an impressive path to success for parents transitioning from foster care to adoption. First, parents will grasp how the system operates, and be properly prepared to cope with what is likely to transpire. Second, parents are encouraged to see life from the child's point of view, understanding the core beliefs and characteristics of children who have had a traumatic childhood. Parents are now able to address presenting issues with wise leadership."

"I particularly appreciated the journal activities Deborah included at the end of each chapter. These impressive exercises, along with the accompanying examples, influence parents to reflect on the concepts addressed prior to starting the next chapter. Deborah lovingly addresses all logistical, legal, and emotional considerations and offers a blueprint for successful foster care adoption.

—Alan Carson, parent educator and coach specializing in adolescence. Alan resides in Pittsburgh, PA and is the author of the award-winning book *Before They Know It All: Talking to Your Tweens and Teens About Sexuality,* published in 2010

"This insightful author guides you through your journey of adoption with compassion and humor. Deborah offers a fresh perspective based upon her family's personal experience as well as her professional training as a parent educator and coach for parents. Deborah wrote this step-by-step guide to help parents find the resources they need and to guide them through the agencies and legal requirements. Better yet, her words capture the essence of every parent's tenderness, anxiety, and excitement. Her words provide emotional support and optimism for every reader. This book is an excellent resource and highly recommended for anyone considering the adoption process."

—Dr. Caron Goode, author of *Nurture Your Child's Gift* (2008), the award-winning *Raising Intuitive Children* (2009), and *Kids Who See Ghosts, guide them through fear* (2010)

"Deborah Beasley's *Successful Foster Care Adoption* is a must read for anyone considering adopting a child. It is a very accurate description of the challenges faced by parents who are considering state adoptions. Written by someone with first-hand experience, it is full of practical advice and wisdom. She tackles tough issues such as childhood trauma, trust, and transracial adoptions in a sensitive but realistic manner. The questions posed to parents throughout her book are insightful. This book fills a long-standing need and will help parents and the children they adopt develop the bonds that will contribute to the building blocks of an emotionally healthy relationship."

— David Handelman, ED. D. Psychologist and clinical director at The Regional Enrichment and Learning Center, New Jersey

"I find the book to be a useful tool that will provide valuable guiding information and encouragement to parents! *Successful Foster Care Adoption* gives an in-depth look at the foster care adoption process. Every aspect of the process is addressed and information given to help parents meet any challenge they may encounter. This book is easy reading with a personal touch!"

    — Shirley Robinson, grandparent caregiver, New Jersey

"This book should be mandatory reading in every state for any parent considering adoption! From the first paragraph, Deborah Beasley had me hooked! It is a powerful, beautifully written and deeply felt book. *Successful Foster Care Adoption* is overflowing with valuable tools, suggestions and specific details for anyone beginning their journey or already involved in the adoption process. She skillfully combines both emotional and practical tools that will help adoptive parents deal with the challenges and obstacles that can arise during and after the adoption process, especially those the parents might not have foreseen. Beasley's personal experience and training combine in the book into an invaluable opportunity for adoptive parents to start off on the right foot. I especially valued the introduction of mindfulness as a key tool in managing stress for both parents and children. I highly recommend this book to parents, educators or counselors working in the field of foster care and adoption."

    —Dr. Minette Riordan, ACPI Certified Coach for Parents and
    Publisher of North Texas Kids Magazine

"Having worked in "The System" for 20 years, there is so much language and law that we know and take for granted. Deborah Beasley has taken the complexities of foster and adoptive parenting and made them humanly possible and understandable. Deborah has created a road map to guide adoptive parents on a successful path of parenting their children. Whether parents are having a tough time or doing well, this is the book they need to read!"

—Deanna L. Davis, M.A., Executive Director, Court Appointed
Special Advocates (CASA) For Children of CGS, Inc.

"As a child protective services worker, we are not privy to the day to day emotions foster/adoptive parents go through. Ms. Beasley has captured the happiness, sadness, frustration and humor of becoming a foster/adoptive parent. It is insightful and moving. A definite read for anyone considering adoption or being a foster parent."

—Daneisha A. Ballard, New Jersey

"This is a book anyone thinking of adopting needs to have! We are foster and adoptive parents and I wish we had this book to guide us during our adoption process. Reading this years later, I continue to find this information enlightening and beneficial. This book clearly helps parents explore the issues in a personal way, and brings out topics that are sometimes missed or avoided. It gives the right information for those wishing to adopt to make the decision of a lifetime."

—Sue LaPierre, Foster and adoptive parent, New Jersey

"Deborah Beasley gracefully combines her personal experiences and professional expertise to provide families in every stage of the foster-to-adopt process with the vital information needed to complete this process successfully. Her guidance is offered in a compassionate, transparent manner. All prospective and current foster-to-adopt parents should read this book!"

—Dr. Diana Saunders, Psy.D Child and Family Therapist
With expertise in developmental trauma, Pennsylvania

Successful Foster Care Adoption

Emotional Journey, Uncommon Love

Successful Foster Care Adoption
A Guide to State Adoption & Parenting Adopted Children

Deborah A. Beasley, ACPI CCPF

ISBN: 978-1-936214-79-2

Library of Congress Control Number: 2012935380

Together At Last Family Press

Published by Together at Last Family Press,
Imprint of Wyatt-MacKenzie

For more information or to order additional copies:
togetheratlast@wyattmackenzie.com

NOTE: Names and other identifying characteristics of individuals in scenarios described in this book have been changed to protect their privacy.

Dedication

For all parents and those soon to be,
whether by birth or by design,
that your journey to family becomes the path
through which you discover the unfathomable depth,
breadth and strength of a love that knows no boundaries.

To my husband, Philip,
my children, my step children and all their spouses,
and to my grandchildren
you inspire and complete me.

NOT FLESH OF MY FLESH, NOR BONE OF MY BONE
BUT STILL MIRACULOUSLY MY OWN

TABLE OF CONTENTS

CHAPTER ONE
REGION: You Are Here
Chapter one is your personal foster adoption workbook. Discusses the importance of getting your emotional bearings as your journey begins. Presents critical points to determine readiness for the foster adoption process.
Back Up & Restore
Manage the Emotional Adoption Roller Coaster

CHAPTER TWO
TRIP PLANNER: Roadside Drive-ins
Discusses the function of the Child Placement Review Board and the Law Guardian as a supportive influence in the foster-adoptive process.
Back Up & Restore
Good Documentation Equals Peace of Mind

CHAPTER THREE
WAYPOINTS: Understanding the Lingo
Presents a brief glossary of foster and adoption legal terminology.

CHAPTER FOUR
TRIP COMPUTER: How Long is Long?
Addresses the emotional impact parents can expect during the wait from placement to finalization.

CHAPTER FIVE
POINTS OF INTEREST: Building Bridges of Effective
Communication
Introduces strategies to develop effective interpersonal
understanding and communication skills when working
with caseworkers and state agencies.
Back Up & Restore
The Self-Healing Art of Mindfulness

CHAPTER SIX
TRAFFIC OPTIONS: Parent Training,
Education, and Support Groups—Oh My!
Offers candid and valuable information to parents and
caregivers to find and establish networks of continued
supportive and educational services.
Back Up & Restore
Spotlighting Children's Mental Health
Empowering Families from the Inside Out

CHAPTER SEVEN
INTERSECTIONS: Lessons in Transition, Trust, and Love
Discusses challenges faced by children coming from foster
care to adoption, and offers methods for successful
parenting.
Back Up & Restore
6 Actions of Remarkable Parents

CHAPTER EIGHT

ALTERNATE ROUTE: Trauma, Stress, & Attachment

Presents research on the impact of trauma and stress, and offers parents strategies for helping children heal through understanding and connection.

Back Up & Restore

Not In My House!

Closing the Door on Reactive Parenting

CHAPTER NINE

HONORING CULTURE IN TRANSRACIAL ADOPTIONS

Let The Soul Searching Begin!

Introduces paths to cultural competency in adoption. Discusses issues of racism and prejudice in American society and its effects on transracial adoptees and their parents.

Back Up & Restore

12 Ways to Honor the Culture, Ethnicity, and Heritage of Your Adopted Child

CHAPTER TEN

HOME: You Have Arrived

Offers an inspirational view for waiting families on the finalization of their child's adoption.

Back Up & Restore

Talking to Children About Adoption

Parenting Resources

About the Author

Endnotes

Acknowledgments

Considerable time, research, emotion, and creative energy are funneled into the process of writing a book. In the case of this book it included looking back on my personal journey, and in the process it triggered my own emotional recollections, some of which will never lose their warmth.

My heartfelt thanks and deepest gratitude must first go to my extraordinary husband, Phil, who never complained with doing dishes, helping with laundry, running the kids around, cooking, cleaning up after dinner and telling me how beautiful I looked, while I sat in my bathrobe past 12 noon on any given day typing furiously! Yes, the stereotypical image of an author bent over the keyboard for hours and days at a time with little thought of personal image, for fear you lose a poignant train of thought, is exactly the course I took. Thanks Honey, for unending patience and support!

To each of my dear children and sweet grandchildren, I say, "Mommy and Grandmom is back in the building and will see you now! Let's play!"

To all those who agreed to share a bit of their personal journey with me so I could include it herein, I am eternally grateful for your candid and honest contributions to this work.

Most especially, my gratitude extends to my friend, mentor, teacher, and now my editor, Dr. Caron Goode. You helped me channel what was inside all along. None of this could have been possible without you.

Preface

"The decision to have a child is momentous. It is to decide forever
to have your heart go walking around outside your body."
~Elizabeth Stone, author

Dear Resource and Adoptive Parents,

Adoption is always an emotionally charged decision, a choice not lightly made. A decision reached over the course of many years and for many personal reasons.

You are reading this book because you are currently in the process of deciding to adopt a child from the state in which you live. You may be deciding to adopt a foster child, whether already in your care or not yet placed. Perhaps you have recently finalized an adoption and are looking for additional information to help lead you forward on the journey. Wherever you are on the road, you have the right book in your hands.

Your decision to bring a waiting child into your life will be to them the healing presence they need to become the children they want to be in the childhood they deserve to have. More importantly, you will be to a child the promise of wholeness, the hope of belonging, and the fulfillment of family.

As a former foster parent and an adoptive parent of two, I know you are feeling a mixture of excitement and apprehension. These emotions are similar to the feelings you have when nearing the top of the first drop on a roller coaster. In the thrill of the moment your heart wants to go, but as the car reaches the top and is momentarily suspended before the vertical plunge, your brain questions what in the world you are doing?

To facilitate bringing heart and mind together in this emotional decision, you need information to empower sound decision-making as to whether adoption through the Child Welfare System is the right choice for you. You need information that will educate and prepare you for what to expect from the emotional journey of adopting a child or sibling group from foster care.

Even with the best preparation, you will need continued support and encouragement along the way. This book will help you find it. I present this information in a factual and candid way so you will have enough support to start your adoption journey with confidence.

Statistics from recent years show increases in the number of state adoptions from foster care systems across the United States. The Evan B. Donaldson Adoption Institute is an unbiased not-for-profit organization devoted to improving adoption policy and practice. Their research shows steady increases in state adoptions from 28,000 in 1996 to 50,000 adoptions in 2000.[1] Spurred primarily by changes in adoption legislation and by state incentives from the Adoption and Safe Families Act passed in 1997, some states have doubled their numbers of foster care adoptions in recent years. These changes mean state adoption has become easier to obtain and the wait to finalization is shorter.

While this is good news for parents who seek to adopt domestically, the numbers of children being adopted still fall far short of the numbers of those waiting for adoption.

Research from the Institute notes that between 1999 and 2000 the total numbers of children in foster care in the United States decreased from 581,000 to 556,000, while the numbers of children awaiting homes increased from 127,000 to 134,000. Of those children who were adopted, foster parents adopted 64% or approximately 32,128 children.[2] There is a pressing need for prospective parents willing to consider the adoption option. With the right information, training, and supportive services, you will determine if foster care adoption is right for you.

Your decision to adopt will initiate the most transformative journey of your life. I cannot tell you it will be easy. Success and struggle are closely related. While disrupted families and foster care placements are a necessary action to insure the safety of children, there is a price to be paid. There are children in the system who carry within them unimaginable pain. You must be ready to help them bear it.

Your adoption journey will lead you on uncharted paths. These paths will be exciting, hope inspired, and sometimes more difficult than you imagine. Along the way you will make an extraordinary discovery about yourself and your child. You will discover a cache of internal strength and courage you never knew existed with the power to transform your life. You will discover that the kind of love you need to consciously design and give your foster and adopted child will need to be much more than ordinary love. Your commitment and acceptance to a child will be a revelation to them of what it means to have someone who is willing to fight through this child's pain and teach them how to love with an uncommon and limitless love.

Open your heart and step bravely. The best is yet to come.

Warmly,
Deborah

"Wheresoever you go, go with all your heart."
~Confucius

Introduction

"Life is a journey, not a destination."

We consider adoption to be the journey of a lifetime. And so it is. This is a book about taking the adoption journey.

We travel this road to experience the most fulfilling of human conditions, becoming a parent. We who have been blessed with children set out on this course because we value what we already have, and we are called or driven to participate in a movement much greater than ourselves.

That so many thousands of children around the world are *available* for adoption is a sign of our impoverished humanity. That so many persons around the world open their hearts and homes each year to embrace a few of these children is a lasting testimony to humanity's enduring nobility.

In writing this book I have used the acronym of a GPS, or global positioning system, which is a satellite navigational system to help you find your destination. The chapter titles and metaphors throughout the book utilize the same terminology and options you would see using your cars GPS system. Following several chapters you will see a feature called *Back Up & Restore*. I use this feature to include additional material to help point you in the direction of solid healthy parenting skills, introduce valuable resources, and reinforce ideas presented in the connecting chapter. I suggest starting and keeping a personal journal because journal writing greatly assists in the processing of internal thoughts and emotions. It will be important to keep checking in with how you really feel about the process of the journey on which you are about to embark.

Whether you are in the initial decision process, have already adopted, or you are someone looking to better understand the foster adoption experience, you will find answers for many of your questions in this book. Use this information as a companion to the information and training offered in your state.

The ability to parent well is a process of self-understanding and growth. Foster care and adoption introduces unfamiliar and specific parenting challenges to parents and families. Both prospective and seasoned caregivers find difficulty in navigating through these unique challenges. My hope is that this book helps you address those challenges and sets you up for ultimate success on the journey. Should you start down the wrong road, it will lead you back on course. When conditions are not clear, it will help you find your way. With this book I provide the navigation tools to guide you into your new role as a forever parent.

CHAPTER ONE

REGION
You Are Here

"The greatest explorer on this earth never takes voyages as long as those of the man who descends to the depth of his heart."
~Julien Green, American Author

Imagine yourself traveling far from home on an epic adventure that will change your future and the future of a child waiting to become part of your life. Filled with hope and anticipation you know only the general direction in which to go and are not certain of your final destination. Your confidence comes from knowing you have a competent guide, and that your GPS is charged and leading you in the right direction and soon you will arrive safely home as a family with child in tow. Welcome to your adoption journey.

Chapter one will provide you with the emotional clarity critical to navigating the aspects of fostering and adopting a child into your life that you will encounter on the journey. Emotions fuel the decisions you are about to make and your ability to balance them well will build your foundation for what lies ahead. You also need to have information and facts on what you can expect from this life changing adventure. You will find this information as well in the following chapters. Adopting from the foster-care system can be lengthy and emotionally draining on prospective parents and their extended families. The more you prepare for this future, the smoother your road trip will be.

Knowing where you are now and which roads lead to your destination is most helpful when beginning your journey of adoption from foster care. You want to adopt. That is, you are or were willing to adopt a child biologically not your own.

- What are the influences driving your decision to adopt?

- How can you determine if the right time to adopt is now?

In order to move forward with greater certainty and conviction, personal reflective work needs to be done. Prior life experiences, whether positive or negative in nature, influence our current actions, thoughts, and decisions and shape us into the persons and parents we become. Personal life experiences are powerful contributing factors through which we find direction and focus in our lives. Chapter one is designed as an in-depth personal workbook to help you determine your emotional readiness to adopt.

Considerable time, emotion and energy will need to be devoted to complete each of the exercises below. You may have already answered some of the questions addressed in this chapter while others take you by surprise. I encourage you to not hold back on examining any issue you have not fully explored so that you are prepared for the trip to adoption ahead. Take these opportunities to delve more deeply into your emotions to discover what strengths and resources are at your disposal. In the process of self-examination you realize you are well on your way to creating a new life and family brought together through the miracle of adoption.

The information you gain about yourself in this first chapter will clarify your direction and set the pace for the rest of your journey. You may choose to complete the exercises now, or as you continue reading through the subsequent chapters. You may wish to delay this chapter and return to it after you have completed reading the book, although I encourage you to jump in. With this process of self-discovery you begin your adoption journey. You are here.

Keep a Journal

If you have not yet done so, I urge you to keep a daily journal from this point forward. Journaling helps you reflect on your decisions, see possible outcomes, and review the emotional impact of the journey you are about to take. Keeping a journal can be a treasured record of your personal journey to your child. It allows you to look back on information and on incidents with new eyes and fresh perspectives. It allows you to formulate your goals, clarify the vision of your hoped-for future, and keep your perspective balanced. Adopting *will* be a wild emotional ride that each of you reading this book will deal with according to your personality traits, personal beliefs, and prior life experiences. Keeping a journal assists you to work through conflicts, face personal fears, and gain wisdom and insight into the actions and words of others and yourself. It will assist you in moving forward with conviction. Start your journal today!

Parenting fostered and adopted children can be difficult. Parenting children who have been abandoned, displaced, or mistreated requires parents who can promise their children uncompromising commitment, and an uncommon and limitless storehouse of healing love and acceptance. At the top of your journal write the name Uncommon and Limitless Love, and beneath it write My Adoption Journey. I have every confidence you will be able to develop a foundation for giving your child and yourself this uncommon and limitless love in the time it takes for you to complete this book.

Proceed With Caution

Consider the following critical points. Use your journal to express and record your thoughts and feelings on each point below. If you have a spouse or significant other committed to your life choices, each of you needs to begin a journal by answering this first question. Discuss your independent answers to this and all subsequent questions with each other, and keep a log of your conclusions.

- **Which paths or life events influence your decision and lead you to consider foster care or adoption?**

    Opportunity: Make a list of five or more events you feel have led to this decision. Make a journal entry thoroughly exploring the reasons and motivation behind considering the adoption option. Be honest with yourself.

- **Why do you believe you are ready to adopt a child into your life?**

    Opportunity: Have this conversation with your partner, spouse, or someone who knows you well and whose wisdom and opinions you trust. What do you hope to gain? What fears do you have? What preparations have been made, and what more do you have to know to feel ready?

- **How have you grieved or found healing and peace from a past experience of infertility or miscarriage?**

> **Opportunity**: Write a letter to the child you wanted but could not have. Let whatever pain remains in your heart spill out onto the paper.

The pain of loss due to infertility or miscarriage can linger long after the event, becoming a factor driving a premature decision to adopt. The grieving process allows for the beginning of healing for both body and spirit. The process cannot be rushed or circumvented. Give yourself permission to grieve. Give yourself permission to heal. When you are ready you may wish to burn the letter. The smoke will rise in a symbolic release of the loss and grief you have endured. Now is the time to honor what you feel. (Keep a copy of your letter for yourself if you wish.)

> **Opportunity:** Write ten ways you can find personal life fulfillment, peace, and happiness. (Raising a child may be one of them!)

This is a further opportunity to complete the healing and clearing of the sadness and grief you have held inside for so long. It is important for you to find meaning to your life apart from and before having or raising a child. Children demand much from parents by the nature of their size, neediness and vulnerability and we can only supply their needs if we have learned how to meet our own first.

The joy and excitement of having a child and becoming a parent are closely connected with our internal need for life fulfillment. Infertility or miscarriage can increase feelings of incompleteness or inadequacy. Validating these feelings is important and equal to recognizing that our children do not come into our lives with a responsibility to soothe our hurts or fulfill our needs. They know nothing of these things. Rather, they are dependent on their caregivers to have the ability and sensitivity to meet their many needs for love, nurturing care, and security. As much as you will love your child, you must be responsible for your personal life fulfillment. Are you ready?

Opportunity: Write ten of the most important gifts you will give a child, and why you believe the gifts you choose will be important to your child's future.

This opportunity is not about material goods and presents. This is about intangible gifts, such as, the incalculable gift of emotional stability and what you have learned in life that you would most like to pass on to your child to enrich their life. If you believe your financial security will play an important role in how you raise your child, it is important you include this in your list. Example: Your child will attend a private school.

- **If you are already a parent, have you presented your intention to adopt to your children?**

Opportunity: Your children will play a big role in this life changing decision. Your careful attention to how you prepare them for the addition of a new sibling enables success. How they feel is important. Let them weigh in on all the issues and answer their questions honestly. Consider not taking a child who is older than your youngest child, unless your youngest child is an infant. Consider the natural hierarchy of siblings, whether by birth or adoption, and how they will view themselves in the mix.

• **Are you prepared emotionally and financially? Is the time right for you?**

Opportunity: Choosing to become a parent is about deciding to dedicate a large part of your life, love, energy, empathy, wisdom, experience, time and resources into empowering a child to become a happy well-adjusted adult. Answer this question by looking at current and future financial obligations. Review also how you respond to personal setbacks and difficulties in life. If you feel you need more emotional support during and after adopting, make certain to structure that into the journey as best you can.

Although it is important to have adequate financial resources to raise a child, I wholly believe that this factor should not dominate your decision. My grandmother, who had six children during the depression and used a dresser drawer for a crib always said, "just add a little water to the pot and make it stretch!"

• **Are you 'new' to parenting? Has it been a while since you parented a younger child? Do you have a strong parenting philosophy?**

Opportunity: Revisit your own childhood to look at how you were parented and decide how you want to parent your child. What will be different? What will be the same? Are you willing to amend or change your parenting style to fit the needs of the foster child placed with you? Are you willing to learn new parenting skills necessary to better understand your adopted child's needs?

Opportunity: Begin to design your parenting philosophy. This is a process and it will take time. Speak with other parents you consider role models or mentors for good parenting. Contact a parenting coach to help in the process and bring out the best in you. Discuss possible difficulties and issues relevant to parenting and how you would wish to handle them in the future. This activity will give you a base on which to begin and build.

· **Name any different circumstances which present special challenges to parenting, such as being a single parent without close support, or being a parent with a disability.**

Opportunity: Begin researching available community, state and federal resources. Speak with family members, friends, and Church affiliations that may be able to give any type of short or long term support. You will need to create a strong system of moral, physical, spiritual and perhaps financial support.

Think of your support network as a full bank account, and each resource or person in this account is willing to be called on and counted on to support you. Just knowing the account is full creates assurance and safety for you. Do not be shy about investing your time in seeking the right resources. Do not hesitate to ask for help and alert others that you would like to call on them if necessary.

• **Have you and your partner or spouse discussed your ability to parent a child with particular special needs or challenging behaviors?**

Opportunity: Research various types of special needs in children. Ask yourself what you need to know to parent a child with particular special needs. How might your parenting approach have to change? What type of education in the development of new parenting skills will benefit you the most? What will best prepare you for understanding how to parent a child with psychological or physical special needs?

• **Have you personally known anyone parenting a child with a disability or mental health diagnosis?**

Opportunity: If you do know someone, speak with or interview that person to gain insight into what parenting a child with such challenges is like. If you don't know someone, contact a local support organization for another parent who is willing to share his or her story with you. If you have personal fears or reservations over raising a child with these serious issues or if you are dealing with these types of issues personally it is most important for you to seek as much information as possible before committing to adopt. Don't give up before you have your questions answered.

· **Have you and your partner explored different types of adoptions you would consider, such as an open adoption, sibling group, or transracial adoption?**

> **Opportunity:** Discuss, or list how each option might impact you and your adopted child over the course of a lifetime. This is an opportunity to begin to examine your feelings about adopting transracially or cross culturally. You will find a wealth of information about transracial adoption in chapter nine.

· **Have you spoken with family members and those who would become a support to you during and after the adoption?**

> **Opportunity:** Invite family members and others over to talk about adoption, celebrate family connections, and share treasured family traditions and the importance of their loving support. What are their feelings about you adopting a child? In what ways might they lend support?

Conclusion

What do you need to know to continue on your journey? You will find some of the answers within you, and some in other places. I suggest you repeat the above exercises at different intervals during the coming months and compare how your answers may have changed. This is only the beginning of your exploration of adoption and the continuation of conversations to come. Adoption is a personal path. I encourage you to take the time you need to explore all the issues. Balance emotion with tangible information and it will bring you to the right road.

"When we are sure we are on the right road
there is no need to plan our journey
too far ahead.
No need to burden ourselves
with doubts and fears
as to the obstacles which may
bar our progress.
We cannot take more than one step at a time."

~ Orison Swett Marden, motivational speaker, Author and
founder of Success Magazine

Back Up & Restore

Manage the Emotional Adoption Roller Coaster

The soul searching questions and empowering exercises you addressed in the first chapter have introduced you to the emotional side of deciding to adopt, and I have no doubt you knew it would be emotional before you ever opened this book. It will be difficult at times to maintain your personal balance and outlook on the future because your emotions will get in the way. Let's face it, your emotions led you to begin your adoption journey in the first place, and that is perfectly okay. The process of making the decision to adopt, whether privately or through the state, can envelope you in a cloud of uncertainty, even while you feel certain you want to continue the ride. I want you to be prepared for the emotionally challenging details, realities, and complexities that come with fostering and adopting a child from state care. Here are three ways to help you (and your child) manage your emotions on the adoption roller coaster, so you can step off the wild ride and keep your feet on level ground as you progress toward your ultimate goal of adoption.

Draw from the wealth of personal insight you gained from completing the exercises in chapter one and follow through in your journal.

1. Write your statement of intention for deciding to adopt and keep it visible at all times. Let your uncommon and limitless love for the most promising and secure outcome for your child guide your intention to adopt.

How much honesty about your interest and motivation to adopt can you bring to the table? The reality is there will be twists and drops along the adoption journey, as it is the nature of the beast. The unexpected can hit us hard even when we are prepared. Your purpose is to remember why you began this journey. You began this journey because of love. It may be because of the love you have to give, or the love you hope to find. Either way love is at the center of your decision to adopt. Remember that the kind of love you must define for yourself and your child will need to be uncommon, committed, and limitless, and it will reflect what all true love is meant to be; giving without thought of self, and only for the other; or giving the best of self for the benefit of the other. When you decide to love a child in need with such generosity you can expect a return beyond your calculations. This kind of love is difficult because it means either way you are emotionally involved, and your heart is wide open and vulnerable. Being open and vulnerable means you can easily fall prey to internal doubt and fear when the journey gets rough, and you may get hurt along the way.

By thinking through and creating a strong statement of intention that matches your values, dreams, and goals, you will overcome the fear and doubt on the journey.

I remind you of the quote by Elizabeth Stone at the beginning of the preface of this book: "Making the decision to have a child is momentous. It is to decide forever to have your heart go walking around outside your body." And so it will be.

2. Compare your perception of how much of the journey needs to be about the child, and how much of the

journey is about you? This will help you maintain your perspective and a broad vision of the road ahead.

For as much as you need your adoption dream to be fulfilled, it is a frightened child that stands at the center of the busy intersection. Your child, like an imaginary small figure walking the yellow dividing line of an 8-lane freeway experiences how uncontrollable and unpredictable their life is. He or she understands how unsafe it is to walk the middle of the highway on which they suddenly find themselves. He or she experiences the rushing traffic of caseworkers, supervisors, and resource parents they hardly know, making life-changing decisions about them and placing them far away from their natural family in unfamiliar and uncertain circumstances. This child needs a parent willing to put their life on the line and cross each harrowing lane of the freeway to take him or her to a home filled with safety and security.

The child that is placed with you will need you to be clearheaded and capable of helping them. Your child will depend on you to impart to them the emotional reassurance, self-regulation, and physical safety they now need in their life. They will look to you to help them sort their own conflicting emotions throughout this process. This means developing a keen sense of what your foster or adopted child is feeling. Become more aware of how their experiences have affected them and how that translates into their current thought processes, belief systems, actions, and attitudes. Your new understanding will influence how you think about your child in a new way and implement a more empathetic, compassionate, and attachment-based parenting philosophy.

By comparing what percentage of those on the journey need what percentage of your energy you will

reach a balance in which you and your child will be able to have your emotional needs amply met.

3. Use attunement and mindfulness to establish self-regulation, safeguard your emotional health, and secure all the points of connection between you and your child.

This is a brief introduction to the benefits of practicing attunement and mindfulness in everyday life and at the end of this section I will give you five of the most accessible ways to practice mindfulness and manage stress! With these five ways you can begin to experience the benefits of this practice today. I will be addressing the concept of mindfulness and the importance of attention to breathing again in the *Back Up & Restore* section of chapter five, although I felt it important to place this introduction in the beginning of the book for your immediate benefit.

The term attunement is defined as "a feeling of being at one with another being." View it as an intuitive connection of how you or another person, in this example your child, feels and experiences a particular situation. To be attuned also means to be mindful and mindfulness is a valuable tool to have in your personal and parenting tool kit. What you learn through the practice of mindfulness will enrich your life and the life of the child you will soon meet.

Why is practicing mindfulness important to you as a parent? In Pennsylvania, Philadelphia area family therapist and Clinical Psychologist, Dr. Diana Saunders supports parents in the practice of mindfulness. She says, "Mindfulness in parenting involves creating an open, loving, and non-judgmental space in which one can look at personal behavior." She suggests that in beginning the practice of mindfulness, parents and caregivers come from a place of self-forgiveness and grace. Dr. Saunders says further, "In order to enhance the use of mindfulness in parenting, offer that grace to your children, your spouse, and most importantly to yourself."

The practice of mindfulness enhances the quality of relationships and interactions you have with yourself and others, especially your children, spouse or life partner. By being mindful you are honest about who you are and who you hope to become. In this state of honesty you learn to accept your strengths and inadequacies equally and with inner grace and peace which leads to self-regulation. Acceptance of self and others with internal grace, peace, and self-regulation, will become three of the most significant gifts you will give to yourself and your child both during the journey to adoption and long after your adoption is final. Mindfulness helps you accept and understand yourself first and it opens you to receive the other person, your new child, as they are. This is an important concept in parenting an adopted child since you do not know the child by birth, you are unfamiliar with their personality and temperament traits, and must learn to integrate the unknown elements of their life and origins prior to coming to you. You must discover how you fit together. Acceptance of the other person, your child, where they are now is a good place to begin blending your lives together.

The Most Accessible Ways to Begin Your Mindfulness Practice

Practicing mindfulness is to practice being in the here and now without allowing your mind, or consciousness, to be pulled into the past or pushed into the future. It is you in the here and now...fully present and fully alive.

Mindfulness allows you to face the past with courage, whether it is scarred with pain or caressed with joy, and it gently holds you in the safe haven of the present without allowing you to become overwhelmed with what may or may not be waiting in the future. Imagine being able to give this powerful healing experience each day to your child and experiencing it with them!

I want you to see the five elements below as a wheel with mindfulness at the rim and at the hub. Each element is represented by a spoke on the wheel that leads you to and from the state of mindfulness. You will be happy to find you are already incorporating some of these elements into your life from completing chapter one. They are

1. Mindfulness and Breath
2. Positive Self-Affirmation
3. Full Body Relaxation
4. Visualization
5. Journaling

Why have I chosen these five elements to help you practice mindfulness and manage the stress of the adoption journey? No matter where you are or what you are doing, you have immediate and unlimited access to these five methods to mindfulness. Instant accessibility increases the likelihood you will use one or more of these elements more frequently, and are therefore more likely to benefit from their use.

Notice that all the elements work on helping you regulate your stress from an internal place. Full body relaxation and journaling also combine external activity. All the elements produce emotional healing and regulation. These attributes transform your internal landscape and will transfer to your external environment in the forms of grace and peace. These five elements of mindfulness are essential coping skills you will learn and teach to your child.

Here are brief explanations of each of the practices.

1. Mindfulness and Breath – Use awareness of and attention to your breathing as a medium to bring your mind into the present moment. In the present moment you focus more deeply (meditate) on the thoughts, words, actions, or aspects of an interaction that need your attention. The daily practice of awareness of breath and deep breathing also allows the mind to clear itself of all thoughts and emotions, and settle into a place of quiet grace and peace. The action of purposeful attention to deep breathing in times of stress breaks the cycle of stress escalation in the body and clears the buildup of negative energy. Heightened stress and negative energy leads to such undesirable reactions as yelling at our child or spouse, losing our patience, or becoming so angry that we cross into sarcasm, hostility, and even aggression toward those we love.

2. Positive Affirmation – Positive affirmations tap our buried internal strengths and call them out into the open to override our negative self-defeating voice. You formulate and repeat positive words and phrases that empower you to overcome life obstacles and strengthen resolve.

"We can do only what we think we can do.
We can be only what we think we can be.
We can have only what we think we can have.
What we do, what we are, what we have,
All depend upon what we think."
~Robert Collier (1885-1950)

3. Full Body Relaxation – Learn to release the stored energy in your body by tensing and flexing each muscle independently. Tense each muscle tightly for five seconds and then release the muscle completely to feel the flow of full body relaxation. Begin with the muscles in your hand and move up one side of your body, across your head, neck, shoulders and back, then down the other side, tensing and relaxing all your muscles. Don't forget the muscles in your legs, ankles, and feet. You can accomplish this discreetly anywhere and anytime you become aware of body tension, anxiety, or stress.

"Everything you do can be done better from a place of relaxation."
~Stephen C. Paul

If you are a better person you will be a better parent.

4. Visualization – It is the onslaught of sensory input that takes our bodies and minds hostage by stress. Calming our senses and limiting input plays an important role in bringing us to the point of inner calm. Examples of sensory input are: lighting (artificial or sunlight), noise (ambient, such as from loud music and television or the internal noise of excessive thoughts and worry), extremes of heat and cold, continuous busy activity such as texting, talking on the phone and a failure to let your senses settle into a place of calm and regulation. Visualization is a powerful means to align our body/mind systems toward internal self-regulation. Visualize your ideal place of peace for five minutes. See, feel, hear, and smell every detail. Then bring your consciousness into the present with sharp focus and breathe peace filled mindfulness into the here and now!

5. Journaling – Journaling is a recognized form of self-healing and has been discussed earlier in chapter one. It balances your emotional perspective, and brings real time wisdom and insight into daily words and actions.

As you continue the emotional ride toward adoption you now have a reliable vehicle in which to make the trip. Maintaining emotional balance and managing stress during your adoption journey is as easy as 1, 2, and 3.

Intention
Perspective
Mindfulness

This is only the beginning of your adoption journey and already you have gained so much. As you move forward I want you to know that it is okay to pace yourself. With little exception, there is no timeline pressuring you to decide, no deadline to meet in your life. Remember, no matter how far you intend to travel, you will always have to stop for gas!

Uncommon and Limitless Love
Journal Activity

Make a journal entry describing what limitless love looks like in your life. Define uncommon love in action. Pull an example from your childhood or adulthood of someone who embodied this love for you. Describe how he or she treated you? How did they talk with you or be with you? What was different and uncommon about them that you liked?

Tell how you show uncommon and limitless love to others in your family. What do you look like in action when you love without limits?

C H A P T E R   T W O

TRIP PLANNER
Roadside Drive-ins

Realizing you are on the journey and knowing what you want to visit on the way is like choosing between *shortest distance* for a speedy arrival at your final destination, or *least use of freeways* for easy access to local attractions. Pulling in at a few local attractions will provide you with a rare opportunity to participate in the legal processes affecting your child's adoption journey, and will add to your understanding of how the child protective system works with the judicial system to legally free a child for adoption. Here are three stops you want to make: inquiry and eligibility, the child placement review board, and the law guardian.

Inquiry and Eligibility

In the state of New Jersey, for instance, parents interested in state adoption would make an initial Inquiry to the Division of Foster and Adoptive Family Services (FAFS), which is part of the Department of Children and Families (DCF). The inquiry process includes getting the information about your state's foster-care and resource parent program and adoptive system, meeting eligibility requirements, and completing the application. If you are already a resource-parent, you are familiar with this process. Educate yourself further as to the legal proceedings followed in your particular state.

Inquiry and eligibility are not only part of an interview of prospective adoptive parents by the state; they are also your exploration of whether or not you can be fairly matched with a child from the system. Most children available for adoption today, domestically and internationally, come from some form of foster care or an orphanage situation. Many will share similar circumstances of placement origin. You may request to meet the child before placement. The more contact you can have with the child, the more secure he or she will feel about coming home with you when the time comes. Matched or not, if you have fallen in love with a foster child already in your home, particularly before the termination of parental rights, the emotional roller coaster ride has begun already.

Once you know how to meet your eligibility requirements for becoming adoptive parents in your state, you can take care of the logistical planning and move closer to the goal of bringing a special child into your life permanently.

The Child Placement Review Board

The Child Placement Review Board consists of trained, experienced, and court-sworn community volunteers. The purpose of this board is to become familiar with the cases of each child in out-of-home placement in the county or the tri-county area that has legal jurisdiction over that placement. Their work is to keep the process moving forward with the current court order in mind, reunification with birth parent, a kinship care placement, or toward the termination of parental rights and adoption.

The board provides the Courts with an accurate and impartial account of all that involves a child's welfare. This includes checking documentation of the child's doctor visits for wellness, whether they are up to date on immunizations, attending school, receiving needed services, or whether parental visitation is taking place regularly. The Board can also interview the caseworker, birth parent, foster or resource parent, or law guardian, to assure that all parties are adhering to the plan for permanency. Foster-parents use this opportunity to voice concerns on behalf of their foster child. Remember that you are in the best position to advocate for the child in your care!

The relationship between the CPR Board, Family Court, and Child Protective Services is symbiotic or interdependent. Child Protective Services must notify Superior Court within 5 days of having removed a child from a home. The notification contains all pertinent information for the removal, including all documented efforts by the Division to prevent such a removal. Removal of children from their family of origin is a decision of last resort and is rooted in the ultimate physical and emotional safety of the child or children involved. The notice provided to the court establishes the continuing jurisdiction of the court over the placement of the child.[3] The child is now in the legal custody of the state.

A report is subsequently issued by Child Protective Services to the court within 45 days of placement and the Child Placement Review Board receives it 15 days later. The Division of Child Protective Services has 30 days to create a placement plan for the child and submit it for review to the Child Placement Review Board. The plan is laid out according to state mandate and law and is followed accordingly.

Child Placement Review Boards meet once a month and

individual cases are up for review every 60-90 days. Your attendance at the review is not mandatory, and caseworkers will inform you of the same. They may suggest it is not necessary for you to attend these meetings. However, as a foster or pre-adoptive parent, you will have little opportunity to be involved with any legal proceedings about your child. Therefore, my recommendation is to take advantage of this limited window to involve yourself in this process. I know you seek to gain as much information about your child and their situation as is possible for their sake. These small tidbits of information may help the children fill the gap in knowledge about what happened to them, as they grow older. I urge you to take on an active role as an advocate on your child's behalf. This Board has influence in your child's case and will be able to answer your questions providing that the privacy of other parties involved is maintained.

Personally, my husband and I never missed a review session for either one of our adopted children. We always brought them with us decked out in all their cuteness. Depending on your child's age, you will want to phone the CPR board to inquire whether bringing your child to a meeting is appropriate, as there are discussions of sensitive family information at some meetings. We once participated in a CPR board meeting via teleconferencing while away on vacation! Having served on our tri-county Child Placement Review Board, I can tell you that members are very glad to see how you and your foster-child interact. They are more than happy to hear what you have to say about how the process affects the child placed with you.

Along with the caseworker, or supervisor, the CPR board may be able to assist you in finding solutions to specific issues you are facing with your child. They also appreciate putting a wonderful little face to the name of the child when

discussing a case. You have nothing to fear from this dedicated and concerned Board, whose purpose is to view your
foster child's case with an impartial lens. Do bring pictures!

The Law Guardian

The Office of the Law Guardian provides necessary legal
representation for children involved in the system of care
because of alleged abuse or neglect from a caregiver. The
Law Guardian is an attorney who is specifically trained to
advocate in cases involving children and youth. Your child
will receive a Law Guardian if the case is classified a Title 9,
which refers to the legal complaint alleging abuse or neglect
against a child's caregiver.[4] An abuse or neglect case is also
referred to as an FN case. You will see these letters on copies
of notifications of court proceedings in your child's case.
You will receive the notifications; however, you will not be
permitted to attend any of the proceedings.

A Law Guardian will see to it that the child they represent will have their basic needs met. My daughters' Law
Guardian visited her at our home several times during the
legal proceedings. He asked if we needed any equipment to
add to her comfort, such as a crib, clothing, or stroller. He
helped us to obtain much needed medical assessments and
services by filing a court order that allowed us to secure
services in a timely manner.

The Law Guardian's function is to assist the older child
to understand the terminology used during court proceedings, to represent the child's voice, and as much as possible,
their wishes, in all legal proceedings. He or she will maintain attorney-client privileges when meeting with the
minor child. You can expect your child's law guardian to be
able to see and speak with your foster child in private when

they visit.[5] I remember being struck with the soft-spoken manner and genuine compassion of my daughter's lawyer.

It is important to note that the function of the Law Guardian is only to represent the child. They cannot represent any other party, nor do they represent your state Child Welfare Agency. You can find out more about the role of the Law Guardian by contacting the Office of Public Defender in your county or state and ask for information about The Law Guardian Program.

Conclusion

As you and your foster-child move through the highways, byways, and tunnels of the Foster-Adoption system, there will be no shortage of challenging terminology to decode or decisions to be made. I urge you to keep your eyes on the prize and hope in your heart. Oh yeah! Don't forget to charge the batteries in your GPS!

Back Up & Restore

Good Documentation Equals Peace of Mind

You are now entering a very different terrain than what you have been accustomed to in the past. Documentation will become a priority and a safety net for you and your child on the journey. Develop good documentation habits early in your foster care experience and you will gain peace of mind and a solid record of critical events in your child's life. Here is the 'How To' to help you organize and simplify your efforts.

1. KISS – *and I don't mean the rock group!* KISS stands for Keep It Simple Silly! Simple is good; simple is uncomplicated; simple is easy. *Anyone* can do Simple.

2. Use an inexpensive and common Composition Book or something similar.

You will need to keep your notes in a book which has all its pages attached. Your documentation is primarily for the benefit of you and your child. Don't discount the importance of taking documentation in foster care and adoption. It will assist you in remembering those details that often escape us at times when we need easy recall. Your documentation provides a chronology of events, may be admissible when settling a dispute, and will work to your advantage. In the event your documented information needs to be presented to the court or others, it is important they see no missing pages.

3. Make notations of all interactions with the caseworker, supervisor, and law guardian.

4. Keep a separate composition book to diary visits your child has with birth parents. Document the following items.

- Days of scheduled visitation: times and duration, and notes on observations made by the child's caseworker and shared with you
- Record the times birth parent misses visitation; excuses given or obstacles sited
- Child's reaction or response before, during, and after parental visits
- Be aware that reactions may begin to surface in your child hours or even days before; and hours, days, or a week after the visit. Children process events differently than adults.
- Make notes of all family of origin details you pick up from caseworkers or others involved in your child's case. This may be the only time you will ever hear these small bits of information. You will probably never see them written in any report. Sadly, the continuity of pertinent information about what happens to children in foster care while being shifted through the system, as well as those from foreign adoptions is rarely ever adequately or accurately maintained. Each time children are passed from one stage of the process or one department to another, caseworkers condense thick files to a mere synopsis of the child's life events, and many pieces are lost. These seemingly incidental puzzle pieces; bits of the original story about what took place the night the child was removed, a siblings name here, and aunt's name there ... will prove to be instrumental to piecing together the big picture of your child's fragmented early life.
- Record how your child reacts to being placed with you, or, preparing for and returning from visitation with birth parent.

5. Keep a log and check list of those who transport the child to and from parental visits.
- How are they transported?
- Are they in seat belts or a child car seat?
- What is the condition of the car seat? Is it clean? (My personal pet peeve!)
- Are the restraint straps frayed?
- Is the car seat appropriate for their size and weight?
- Is it facing the appropriate direction for their age?
- Is the car seat secured correctly in the car?
- Does the person transporting the child or children appear competent?
- Exactly where will the child be taken?
- Who will be returning the child to you?
- What time will that be?

Keep in mind the persons who transport your child weekly to visitation ferry many children of all ages back and forth many times in a day. Don't presume they are fully mindful of which car seat they are using for which child, that it is securely attached to the seat, or that the child is correctly in the car restraints. Although this is their responsibility, you will become the overseer.
- Do go out with the child and introduce them to the transporter, who likely is not their caseworker.
- Do take all their pertinent information: Name, organization with which they are associated, cell phone number, and ask to see their I.D.
- Do reassure your child, who most likely views this event as frightening and disrupting, that you will be there when they get back. Their hidden fear is you won't be there or that they will simply not be able to return.
- Do allow them to take something dear to them to

comfort them in this stressful and scary reality. You may have to put their name and your phone number on it so it returns with the child.
- Do be very available to them when they return home. Spend time with them one on one.
- Do allow them to talk about the experience when they are ready.
- Don't burden them with undo questioning, or negative attitudes concerning their family or visitation.

Understand they might become angry, fearful, whiney, clingy, silent, withdrawn, over reactive, highly sensitive, stubborn, defiant, inflexible, or desperately attached at the hip. These are all common reactions in children who feel abandoned, displaced and uncertain of their immediate welfare or their future. As has been stated earlier, sadly, this is the nature of the beast.

6. Record your observations concerning the general mental and emotional health of your child, as you see it.
- Do notice any changing behaviors and/or moods.
- Do become sensitive to what your child is going through, no matter what their age, including infants.
- Children do not understand what is happening and they wonder why such terrible and scary things have happened to them.

7. Record all disputes, causes, and outcomes with anyone involved in your foster child's case.

8. Phone the caseworker or supervisor to try and come to the most agreeable solution for all involved, especially for the child.

9. In your notes include times, dates, involved parties, who they represent, place of meeting, reason for meeting or interaction, the general or specific questions asked, and points made.

Documenting, understanding, and where necessary, sharing important details will help you keep your case-worker informed of your child's levels of need. It will help you both determine the best case plan, make joint informed decisions about possible changes (where it is legal for you to do so), and whether your child may need further care to secure his or her emotional health. Those of you who are new to the foster care-adoption trek may feel as though you are off-roading! Never fear! If you take the time to document all the important stuff, peace of mind will be just around the corner. Your increasing knowledge and confidence will quickly switch you into four-wheel drive no matter what the terrain ahead!

WAYPOINTS
Understanding the Lingo

In my personal adoption journey, I experienced moments, not unlike some of you, when navigating the foster care system became akin to traveling in a strange land where customs, terms, and phrases were as unfamiliar as a foreign language. When in a foreign country one of the best ways to learn the lingo is by pulling into the waypoints and hanging out with the locals.

Some of you will have no prior experience with the sensitive issues you may now have to face during the adoption journey. For others the mere discussion of certain terms in this chapter will bring your most difficult past memories to light once again. Press on, and remember.

> *"Life's challenges are not supposed to paralyze you;*
> *They're supposed to help you discover*
> *who you are."*
> ~Bernice Johnson Reagan, singer, songwriter, scholar

Following are clarifications of common terms you will encounter on the journey. This brief glossary is not meant to be a complete adoption terminology dictionary. Rather, it contains some of the terms, which are apt to be more easily misunderstood by or unfamiliar to resource parents during the adoption process. I have also added terms, which would be of particular special interest to you as caring and loving caregivers. Each state will define some of the following terms differently according to their individual state statutes.[6] The case worker working with your family will be glad to give you additional materials which will further broaden your understanding of the legal terms used in foster care adoption. Just ask!

The following terms are in alphabetical order.

Abandonment - "A situation in which the child has been left by the parent(s), the parent's identity or where-abouts are unknown, the child suffers serious harm, or the parent has failed to maintain contact with the child or to provide reasonable support for a specified period of time."[7]

Abuse or Neglect - The Child Abuse Prevention Act (CAPTA) defines abuse and neglect as "any recent act or failure to act on the part of a parent or caregiver, which results in death, serious physical or emotional harm, sexual abuse or exploitation, or an act or failure to act which presents an imminent risk of serious harm."[8] This definition is not limited to children already born, but is equally applied to pre-born children, such as in cases of pre-natal drug or alcohol exposure.

The Center for Disease Control and Prevention (CDC)[9] lists several definitions of child maltreatment. The CDC divides maltreatment into 'acts of commission' and 'acts of omission.' In the world of Child Welfare there are critical legal distinctions in the terms and definitions that play an important role in determining judicial actions applied to cases of child abuse or child neglect, and it is important for you to understand the differences.

Child Maltreatment is defined as "any act or series of acts of commission or omission by a parent or other caregiver (e.g., clergy, sports coach, and teacher) that results in harm, potential for harm, or threat of harm to a child."[10] Because of the seriousness and importance in accurately interpreting the differences between these acts, I have included the complete definitions below without paraphrasing.

"Acts of Commission" (Child Abuse) – Words or overt actions that cause harm, potential harm, or threat of harm to a child. Acts of commission are deliberate and intentional; however, harm to a child may or may not be the intended consequence. Intentionality only applies to the caregivers' acts, not the consequences of those acts. For example, a caregiver may intend to hit a child as punishment (i.e., hitting the child is not accidental or unintentional) but not intend to cause the child to have a concussion. The following types of maltreatment involve acts of commission: Physical abuse, Sexual abuse, Psychological abuse.

"Acts of Omission" (Child Neglect) – The failure to provide for a child's basic physical, emotional, or educational needs or to protect a child from harm or potential harm. Like acts of commission, harm to a child may or may not be the intended consequence. The following types of maltreatment involve acts of omission:

Failure to provide
- Physical neglect
- Emotional neglect
- Medical/dental neglect
- Educational neglect

Failure to supervise
  • Inadequate supervision
  • Exposure to violent environments"[12]

Background Check - A background check is an investigation of the prospective foster and adoptive parents and anyone else who will be living in the foster child's new household. Background checks include fingerprinting and all subsequent related and criminal record searches at the State and Federal levels. A denial of approval for either the application for adoption, or license of adoptive or foster home, may be issued by the state if it is found that any adult living in the home has been convicted of certain crimes including sexual abuse of a minor.[13]

Best Interests of the Child - When the court is faced with pending actions on behalf of a child under their jurisdiction, the state must make a lawful determination on whether those actions are in the best interest of the child. Some considerations affecting the determination of best interests are whether the proposed actions will result in the permanency and well-being of the child.[14]

Cultural Competence - "The ability of individuals and systems to respond respectfully and effectively to people of all cultures, ethnic backgrounds, sexual orientations, and faiths or religions in a manner that recognizes, affirms and values the worth of individuals, families, Tribes, and communities, and protects and preserves the dignity of each. Cultural competence is a continuous process of learning about the cultural strengths of others and integrating their unique abilities and perspectives into our lives."[15]

Home Study - An accredited home study agency in your state or locality is contracted to conduct the home study activities for prospective resource, kinship and adoptive families. In a variety of activities, evaluations, home visits and inspections the agency will determine the suitability of the prospective resource home and family. The agency will also make determinations necessary to match children with those families who might best meet their needs.[15]

Life Book - It is strongly suggested and sometimes mandatory to build a Life Book for your foster child. Request information from books already in existence, or start one of your own. Gather as much information about your child's past experiences, placements, schools, friends, foster-parents and siblings as you can. Enlist help from his or her caseworker or Law Guardian to fill the blanks. Consider these 3 sources for information.

- Any portion of hospital records, such as the newborn's footprints. I am fortunate to have the page from our second daughter's birth records that has her actual newborn footprints.

- Photographs. I was able to get photos taken by the first caseworker and second foster family who had my child.

- Written narrations by those with knowledge of your child's past. Former foster parents or teachers are happy to do this.

It is critical for you to place importance and urgency upon building a life book for your foster or potential future adopted child. From their stark reality of loss and disconnection and often being too little to remember what happened to them, your efforts may hold the sum of their young lives and become a precious link with their past. Do it for them.

Permanency Plan and Concurrent Planning - The ultimate goal of family intervention by child welfare is to assist in the stabilization of the family and return the child from foster care or temporary state custody to their family of origin. All efforts are made by the state to work with birth parents toward reunification.

Simultaneously, an alternate and time sensitive plan is made to provide permanency for the child in the event reunification does not take place.

Concurrent Planning includes securing a prospective relative care or adoptive home. The state will actively pursue all reasonable options for permanency for the best benefit of the child. The Permanency Plan and Concurrent Planning will take place during the same time period and with full knowledge of all parties involved: natural parents, pre-adoptive family, and the child if he or she is old enough.

Placement Identification Letter - Upon placement of a child in your approved foster or pre-adoptive home, you will receive a Resource Parent Identification Letter. This letter contains specific information about you and your foster child:
- Child's name
- Gender
- Date of birth
- State ID number
- Medicaid number

· Name of foster parent
· Address/phone number and placement date

The letter will include what foster parents are lawfully authorized to do for the child:
· Register child in school
· Work with school to develop an appropriate curriculum, such as an IEP (Individualized Educational Plan)
· Consent to medical/dental/therapeutic/pharmacy services for the child, if considered routine care
· Obtain other social services

The above information has been taken from the Resource Parent ID letter. Review all the information in your letter carefully for accuracy. Contact the child's case-worker to make changes. Carry this document with you at all times when with your foster child. Keep the original with your records and a copy with you. To obtain services or testing and to prove the child is legally in your care, you will have to produce this document. The Placement Identification Letter is generally valid for a period of six months, at which time a new letter will be issued by the state.

Special Needs Children - Classifications in each state may differ and are typically broad in interpretation. This list is not complete and categories can include:
· Medical/physical conditions
· Mental health/behavioral conditions
· History of parental drug use
· History of trauma through abuse/neglect
· History of multiple foster care placements
· Age of child
· Race of child
· Gender Orientation

Temporary State Custody - When the court has found cause and legal justification for abuse Child Protective Services removes the child from the home and places him or her in the temporary custody of the state. This usually means placement in the approved home of a grandparent, other relative, resource or foster parent.

Termination or Severance of Parental Rights (TPR) - The Termination of Parental Rights is a legal action taken by the Court without the consent of the birth parents to legally remove their right to raise their child. This action is a judicial move to clear the child for the possibility of adoption by an approved foster family or kinship caregiver.

Supervised Visitation - Birth parents have the right to see and speak with their children unless otherwise restricted by the state. Visitation will take place by court order and may stipulate supervision by a caseworker or affiliate agency worker. Supervision means that the worker will be present with the child and natural parent during the scheduled visit. Grandparents or siblings can be involved in regularly scheduled visitations.

Conclusion

Terminology can appear confusing and foreign, with the potential to lead us down a dark, uncharted road. Fear lives in what is unknown and misunderstood. Marie Curie said it this way, "Nothing in life is to be feared. It is only to be understood." Once you fully understand the lingo, you proceed on course with certainty and confidence. Knowledge is power, Baby!

TRIP COMPUTER
How Long Is Long?

*"We must let go of the life we have planned, so as to accept
the one that is waiting for us."*
~Joseph Campbell, writer

How long before my child is legally free for adoption?
How long until our family is together at last?
How long is long?

Like billboards along the roadside, these questions
obscure our ability to see the broader view. The issue is not
that there are questions, rather, how we ourselves will give
the answers. How long will it take? Your response is: *SOON*.

My husband is fond of saying, "How long is a piece of
string?" The answer to each listed question is relative.
According to the most recent published study, there are
approximately "126,000 children in foster care awaiting
adoption in the United States."[17] Each child has his or her
own personal story. For each of these children the answer
to the question of how long is unique. In the vast numbers
of those who seek to adopt, each parent also enters the
journey with their trip computers running and their own

matchless stories. Together and yet still apart, both child and parent enter this waiting time with unparalleled hope for their future as a family.

Stages to Finalization

Each state has established stages in the process from foster care to finalization of adoption and beyond. For your convenience, I have included an outline of these stages here.

"A. Entry Stages
    1. Identify placement
    2. Finding of abuse or neglect
B. Permanency Planning
    1. Initiate concurrent planning
    2. Establish/change goal
    3. Hold Hearing
C. Termination of Parental Rights (TPR)
    1. Diligent search
    2. Conduct TPR proceedings
    3. Provide legal services
    4. Conduct proceedings for appeal
D. Adoptive Placement
    1. Recruit adoptive home
    2. Select adoptive home
    3. Approve adoptive home adoption
    4. Establish adoption subsidy/services
    5. Prepare/transition child and family
E. Post Adoption Stage
    1. Provide post-adoption services"[18]

The reality is that each stage takes months to accomplish. You are a bystander in the Entry Stages. The phone call requesting child placement may have been made to five other foster parents before you, but you will not be aware of that. You will say yes based on personal reasons and a deep intuition which tells you *this is the one.*

The Waiting Time

The longest portion of the journey will be between concurrent planning for permanency and the TPR appeal process. The birth parents will be under court orders to follow certain actions, which, if completed, will result in the reinstatement of custodial rights. It means the child will be returned to their care. In some cases the birth parents will be ordered to attend a drug or alcohol program, counseling, parenting support program, or to obtain adequate housing. State Child Welfare Agencies and the court will allot *repeated* amounts of time for birth parents to effect change in their lives and accomplish these goals.

Keep in mind that a birth parent has 45 days to appeal a court ruling. They have the right to get their own attorney or have one appointed. And they can and do fight to retain rights to their children.

According to extensive research conducted by the 2004 release of the Urban Institute Child Welfare Research Program entitled, *Foster Care Adoption in the United States, A State by State Analysis of Barriers and Promising Approaches,* significant barriers to addressing the issues of effectively managing and improving case planning and timely adoptions for children in state care have been noted in most states.

The research results list the following top five barriers to moving a child toward adoption in a timely manner. Each of the five categories where barriers were most often identified is also listed above in the Stages to Finalization.

Top Five Barriers to Timely Adoptions

1. Conduct TPR Proceedings – 48 states reported barriers under this heading that delays the adoption process. Some of the barriers cited were, insufficient services to birth parents in helping them effect change and reestablish their lives, and reluctance by the court and agency to terminate parent's rights before an adoptive family could be identified.

2. Recruit Adoptive Home – 47 states reported difficulties in finding sufficient adoptive homes for waiting children.

3. Child Welfare Case Management – 43 states reported significant barriers in case management, including incomplete case records, and delays in transferring cases from ongoing case units to the adoption unit.

4. Court Case Management – 43 states reported barriers in case management in various areas, from the judicial beliefs about adoption to continuances and docket overloads.

5. Establish/Change Goal – 42 states reported delays in the adoption process due to issues such as, maintaining the goal of reunification too long and neglecting to consider adoption early enough in the case process.[19]

Notwithstanding the boundaries and time limits set for achieving permanency by the Adoption and Safe Families Act (ASFA), the length of time it takes to complete this leg of your journey home will be founded upon particular nuances of your child's case history. You equally understand a few of the issues and difficulties faced by Child Welfare Agencies and judicial systems across the United States which affects the completion of the adoption process for every child and parent traveling toward the goal of family. The struggle is mentally exhausting and emotionally draining. Both sets of parents are in the throes of labor at the same time. Birth parents labor in an attempt at rebirth, and pre-adoptive parents labor to birth their dreams of a family into reality.

Below I share an entry from my own adoption journal. In the journal I speak to my future child, narrating the story of our journey. By this sharing, I join with each of you in this waiting time.

Adoption Journal Entry, May 23, 2000

My dear child,

Sometime late in 1999, I came across a very small ad in the newspaper. An agency was looking for six couples interested in adoption to participate in a brand new program called Fost-Adopt. Your Daddy didn't know I had cut it out and put it secretly in my drawer. In February 2000, we went to classes to see for ourselves what the program was about. Our journey has begun.

Now we wait for you. Now we wonder where you are. Are you born yet? Are you a boy or girl? How old are you? Are you safe?

Everything is ready for you. The whole family is ready for you. *Soon* we will see you. *Soon* we will meet you. *Soon* we will hold you.

Conclusion

How long will it take to complete the process from placement to adoption? How long is a piece of string? The exact length the process of adoption is for your family will have an answer as uniquely different as the child and their circumstance. Although you will find the waiting difficult, the anticipation and joy of your dream will keep your arms open until they wrap snuggly around the right child for you.

Uncommon and Limitless Love
Journal Activity

You have been waiting, wondering and hoping for so long. You have spent countless hours imagining how your dream will come to fruition. You have been imagining your child and your family.

Write a letter in your journal today about your waiting time. Write to your future child all you would tell him or her if you were face to face now. If you have been thinking about choosing a name for your future child, use that name now. Even if you decide to keep the child's birth name, or change it later, choosing a special name for your child now will nourish the small fragile seed of attachment already planted in your heart.

Tell your child the story of what you are going through, like what you feel, all you hope for, and the fears you have if the journey does not happen as you expect. Encourage your spouse or partner, grandparents or siblings to compose their own letters expressing their anticipation of a new family member and all the preparations being made for the arrival.

In the years to come you will look back on these letters with renewed love, insight, and strength. Perhaps you will add these letters to your child's life book. Perhaps you will choose to read your letter to your child when they become older or at special occasions as a legacy of when your love for them began. Take time now to write to your child.

CHAPTER FIVE

POINTS OF INTEREST

Building Bridges of Effective Communication

"To effectively communicate, we must realize that we are all different in the way we perceive the world and use this understanding as a guide to our communication with others."
~Anthony Robbins

Your building bridges of effective communication with caseworkers, supervisors, children, and even your spouse is the foundation for a strong relationship. When involved in an emotional endeavor such as foster-care and adoption there is bound to be miscommunication. How can you build good communication skills so you can avoid missing the bridge and keep from falling into the miscommunication ravine? Take the following scenario in point.

Sharon is a foster mom hoping to adopt her two young sibling charges who have been in placement with Sharon for 19 months. Like any waiting adoptive mom, Sharon is anxious for the process to reach completion. She is very much in love with the children and becomes fearful that the process may not go through to the adoption. The children's case is complicated by many factors and after several delays; Sharon fears the worst when their caseworker visits with news.

Because of her fears Sharon is under stress when the caseworker comes to call. On this particular afternoon her four-year-old is home from nursery school, has been up much of the night, and feels miserable with a bad cold. Sharon received a letter from the home inspection office stating several things she will need to change or fix in the house before she can pass inspection and maintain her foster parent open-home status, which she will need in order to adopt.

Shortly after reading the letter Sharon finds a message on her answering machine that the caseworker is in the neighborhood and wishes to stop by. Against her better judgment, and wishing to be polite and cooperative, Sharon phones the caseworker to say it's all right for her to come. Sharon's internal stress levels escalate. By the time the caseworker arrives, Sharon is not in the best of moods and regrets telling her to come.

The caseworker informs Sharon there is yet another complication in the process of Sharon adopting the children. A relative has recently been identified who may be suitable to raise the children. An investigation as to whether the placement will be viable and safe is happening now. She tells Sharon she will have to persevere a while longer. Sharon was already tired and close to a boiling point before the caseworker arrived. Now all of Sharon's conflicting emotions spill over. She proceeds to unload all her real feelings to the caseworker about how slowly the case is proceeding, the unreasonable and ever changing demands placed on her by the home inspection office, and how the children are being mistreated and manipulated unfairly by the state.

The caseworker flatly explains the legality of the issues

involved in a relative search, and furthermore, that Sharon should have been aware of the risks involved before she became a foster parent. Sharon is overwhelmed and unceremoniously tells the woman to leave. The caseworker is insulted and leaves, but informs Sharon that her reaction could result in the removal of the children. This statement is a further threat to Sharon who is emotionally invested in the children and their well-being.

The altercation with the caseworker now increases Sharon's fears about losing the children. The caseworker leaves angrily, questioning Sharon's ability to continue with the placement. The caseworker may be unaware of Sharon's fearfulness and perceives her reaction as an impatient angry outburst. Sharon now wonders how to best relate to the children. Perhaps it is best that she protects herself emotionally from a greater hurt of losing the kids whom she has grown to love so dearly. Perhaps she should be more aloof so they learn not to be so attached to her, especially if they will be disrupted and placed with yet another family. Sharon now feels her path darkened and confused.

Having been a foster parent for 6 years and involved in support groups, related boards, and associations for 13 years, I know emotions run high in foster and pre-adoptive parents. Communication suffers. In the previous scenario Sharon has all the right intentions to follow through with the requested meeting but fails to follow her intuition. In addition, Sharon's real feelings and fears were brought into the open by the strong statements used by the caseworker. It might have been a better decision to postpone the meeting until

- Sharon was rested and calmed.
- Sharon's daughter was feeling better and back in school.
- Sharon had given herself time to process her issues or

objections over the home inspection letter.

- Sharon had the opportunity to share and vent her feelings with a spouse, partner, friend, or support person.
- Sharon had her spouse, partner, or support person help her gain new perspectives on her fears and emotions and how they immediately affect her and her children.

Mutual Trust & Respect

The underlying core issue in the inability to communicate effectively is the lack of mutual trust and respect.[20] Without trust and respect, only fear and distrust of others' motives and intentions are left. Without trust and respect between parties, it is nearly impossible to find good solutions to effective communication. Distrust is the foundation then.

In Sharon's story, both the caseworker and Sharon are concerned for the well-being of the children. The caseworker and Sharon view their situation from very different perspectives. There are two primary issues for each to address:

- The buildup of Sharon's daily stressors
- Sharon's misunderstanding that stems from unfamiliarity with the system
- The caseworker's pressures and concerns of a stretched caseload
- The caseworker's emotional toll of working in the Child Protective Services profession.

Beyond these points is a deeper issue that is difficult to ignore. The sum result of prior negative experiences and long-held assumptions between state workers, the organizations they represent and resource parents have created a cloud of mistrust. The warranted concern is a challenge for parents and state workers to continuously overcome. In the broader perspective, the mistrust lies between the foster parent and the state's Child Welfare Agencies.

The invisible elephant in the room is past and current gross inadequacies of Child Welfare Agencies across the United States, the systemic failure to provide appropriate protection to children in their care, and in the screening, training, and continual supervision of physically and emotionally safe resource and adoptive homes. My purpose is not to address these issues in this book, but it is important to recognize what underlying barriers create mutual mistrust and lack of respect between parties.

Much work has been accomplished at state and federal levels to identify and address barriers faced by agencies throughout the states.[21] Much work is yet to be done. Alabama began its reform of their Child Welfare system as part of a landmark settlement (RC vs. Hornsby) in 1991.[22] In June of 2002, it was noted that Alabama child welfare reform "was the first reform to be driven not by procedural requirements but by the principles of good practice."[23]

Partnership with all parties and meeting the child's needs for stability and family integrity were key principles, as were working from a model of strength and need of both child and family. "When all involved agree ... on what a child needs, and undertake to do whatever is necessary in order to meet those needs, more intensive services are provided that result in shorter stays in foster care placement and adoptions that do not break down."[24]

Over the years I have witnessed the beginning of reform in my own state.

The changes are a beginning and efforts are ongoing. Weaknesses in the systems of care still exist and legal and child advocacy groups must remain vigilant in holding states responsible for the safety and health of every child placed in their care.

As a potential resource parent and adoptive parent, you bring your strengths of good moral character and genuine love and care for the safety and welfare of children to the table of reform in your state. You can decide to join with thousands of dedicated resource parents and social workers to become a positive asset, model, and inspiration in the lives of a child or children placed in your care.

Our awareness of the problems must not impede our progress forward or threaten to overwhelm us into inaction. After all...how do you eat an elephant? One bite at a time!

How We Say It Makes A Difference?

"The most important ingredient we put into any relationship is not what we say or what we do, but what we are."
~Steven Covey

That is not to say there is no merit to what we say or how we say it. Communication is much more than vocal expression. We interpret a lot of meaning from body posture, gestures, facial expressions, and overall body language. At our core, who we are will become evident to those around us if we are mindful and genuine in the way we communicate.

The following 8 touch points will bridge the communication gap you experience and help make your road a little smoother.

8 Points of Good Communication

- Ask for and give mutual trust and respect at the beginning of interactions with others.

- Express your expectations and hear the expectations of others.

- Listen attentively and with empathy to the concerns of others in the conversation.

- Voice your concerns clearly and calmly.

- Ask questions to get clarification of issues you don't understand.

- Identify at least one positive aspect in the interaction to help you keep negative emotions from flaring.

- See the situation from the others viewpoint as you both work toward solutions and mutual understanding.

- Honor what is important and right and always be true to your core values.

Following are a few tips to help you effectively prepare for any type of communication. These points have served me well in the past, and I frequently share them with parents I work with. I have used these tips to prepare for IEP meetings, when speaking with family therapists, and at team case management meetings. I consider the points below to be universally beneficial for their ease of use and versatility in many situations.

a) State your concern briefly

b) Request a mutually convenient time to discuss the issue

c) Make bullet points on what you want to say to stay on track

d) Don't assume you understand the answers, repeat what you think you understand back to the other party for confirmation

e) No matter how upsetting your concerns, keep negative emotions in check. No one wins when communication 'goes south'

f) If you feel unheard or disrespected state your perception with an "I" statement, such as:

- "When ... I feel... because."

- *"When* I hear your message, *I feel* upset and stressed; *because* I am afraid the adoption won't go through."

- Or, "*When* you call early for a meeting, *I feel* relieved; *because* I have more time to prepare for what I wish to speak about."

g) Don't forget to take notes of the conversation or interaction including the date. Stress can play havoc with our ability to remember facts accurately.

h) Follow up by putting it in writing. If it is an important issue, send a follow up letter (Return Receipt Requested) or email restating the highlights and conclusion of the conversation.

The Center for Nonviolent Communication

The Center for Nonviolent Communication is a world-wide non-profit organization. Theirs is a rich philosophy of Compassionate Communication. The NVC model uses four components of Observation, Feelings, Needs, and Request to create connection and deep understanding within each human interaction. These four components are four pieces of information through which we communicate more effectively with others, and they with us.

Nonviolent communication does not depend upon the other person knowing the four components. Whether we are in a conflict situation or simple daily life conversations, our ability to articulate what we are observing, feeling, needing, and requesting in that moment enables the other person to be enabled to do the same. True compassionate communication attunes us to the feelings and needs of another with the sole intention of enriching his or her life. When we communicate clearly, the needs of both parties are met.

You Can Do These Ten Activities to Contribute to Internal, Interpersonal, and Organizational Peace.

1. Spend some time each day quietly reflecting on how you would like to relate to others and yourself.

2. Remember that all human beings have the same needs.

3. Check your intentions to see if you are as interested in others getting their needs met as your own.

4. When asking someone to do something, check first to see if you are making a request or a demand.

5. Instead of saying what you DON'T want someone to do, say what you DO want the person to do.

6. Instead of saying what you want someone to be, say what action you would like the person to take that you hope will help the person be that way.

7. Before agreeing or disagreeing with anyone's opinions, try to tune in to what the person is feeling and needing.

8. Say what need of yours prevents you from saying yes instead of saying no.

9. If you are feeling upset, think about what need of yours is not being met, and what you could do to meet it, instead of thinking about what's wrong with yourself or others.

10. Instead of praising someone who did something you like, express your gratitude by telling the person what need of yours that action met.[25]

Conclusion

Effective communication in relationship is like building a bridge of mutual understanding. We observe the dynamics of each interaction without falling into the ravine of negative emotion. We place ourselves in the shoes of the other which opens us to their feelings and needs in the moment. We articulate requests, instead of demands, in order to best affirm and enrich our own life and that of others and certainly the lives of our children. On the bridge of communication, understanding extends the steel girders of trust. Trust becomes the bolts of confidence. Confidence is the paved highway of hope. Hope leads to promise. Promise turns into safety and reassurance on the other side of the ravine, where the communication bridge meets solid ground again.

Back Up & Restore

The Self-Healing Art of Mindfulness

"You cannot find yourself by going into the past.
You can find yourself by coming into the present."
~Eckhart Tolle

By deciding to take the high dive into foster care adoption, you are also willingly diving headlong into what is, for some, an undeniably high stress situation. In these waters you are not alone. Within the tidal wave of increasing daily pressures it is no wonder we frequently find ourselves exhausted and out of breath. The tsunami-like surge of modern day demands and the frenzied technologically-driven pace of twenty-first century life threatens to take its toll on kith and kin.[26] If this describes you or your family, don't despair. The answer is clear and beautifully simple; practice the self-healing art of mindfulness; the art of coming up for air.

How Long Can You Hold Your Breath?

In June 2001 Brazilian free-diver Karoline Meyer[27] set the world record for women's breath hold. She voluntarily held her breath underwater for 6 minutes and 13 seconds. Eight years later, according to the Guinness Book of World Records, on July 10, 2009, Karoline again broke a new world record holding her breath under water for an inconceivable 18 minutes and 32.59 seconds.

While the above statistic seems too fantastic for some to believe, many persons, foster and adoptive parents included, find themselves passing through life holding their breaths. Over-scheduling, once common only in doctors' practices, is now the norm in every household. Families barely function without synchronizing the daily planners of each member. Important life choices are often rushed or made in hindsight instead of the light of forethought. We are submerged in the doing, accomplishing, and filling of every moment with little thought to its residual effects on mind, body, and spirit.

An argument can be made that modern humans live in a self-perpetuating state of emotional, physical, and spiritual suffocation. We exist in fleeting glimpses of consciousness with only vague awareness of the present moment.

Yet, it is precisely within the present moment that we live and are most fully alive.[28] In the present moment, the here and now, we can experience the fullness of life in every aspect of our lives, including the way we parent our children and interact with others. How long can you hold your breath in an effort to keep pace with life?

A Legacy of Stress

We live in a culture of stress. According to a study in 2010 by the American Psychological Association, "One third of all Americans believe they are living in extreme stress." In fact, high stress is one of the leading causes of health problems in the United States.[29] Where is your family in this mix?

Facts on Stress - The latest survey statistics by the American Psychological Association have found:
• Work related stress affects 70% of Americans (APA poll 2010)

- 73% of Americans suffer significant stress related to the economy (APA poll 2004)
- 66% of Americans report actively seeking help to manage their life stress (APA poll 2004)
- More children and adolescents are diagnosed with stress related disorders every year

According to information by the National Institute of Mental Health (NIMH), an estimated 40 million people are now affected by anxiety disorders each year.

Effects of Stress on the Body
- Headache
- Shortness of breath
- Inability to think clearly
- Sleeping too much or too little
- Overeating or not eating enough
- High blood pressure
- Anxiety attacks
- Digestive problems
- Gut-related disorders like Irritable Bowel Syndrome
- Feelings of Depression and Isolation
- Stress interferes with our ability to maintain healthy relationships with our partners, children, co-workers, and friends.
- Stress prevents us from being healthy and whole persons.

Recently I sat with a mom who lamented feeling fragmented and burnt out by family over-scheduling. "I ran into an old friend the other day," she said. "She asked why she hadn't seen me lately at my daughter's dance practices. Sadly, this was the answer I gave her."

"Life is crazy for us," she explained. "My husband works

rotating shifts. One week he's on nights; the next week he's on days, and the next he works in the afternoons. I work a few afternoons to help make ends meet. We switch off doing the food shopping, laundry, and picking the kids up from school. We have five calendars on the refrigerator, one for each of us. Between our work schedules, taking care of the house, the kids' sports, and karate and piano lessons … " she heaved a deep sigh without finishing the list. "We are both exhausted! There is so much to do. If it's not on the calendar, we don't remember to do it! But, what can you do?"

Then she answered her own question, "This is what you have to do to live life these days."

Is the above observation true, or can it be a matter of choice? Can you choose to slow the pace of life enough to catch your breath and restore essential life energy? The daily practice of Right Mindfulness will help you find peace, balance, and harmony, even amid stressful times.

A Return to Ancient Wisdom

"We are not human beings on a spiritual journey.
We are spiritual beings on a human journey."
~Steven Covey

In modern times, barriers between cultures and religions are less defined and more open than in previous decades. With the introduction of Transcendental Meditation[30] in the late 1960s and '70s, Eastern religious practices and philosophies have steadily grown in influence in Western society. In the turbulent climate of the '60s and '70s, even meditation was viewed by some as a threatening intrusion to our established and constrained Western civilization.

Today many Americans have incorporated Eastern ideologies into their daily lives. Yoga, Reiki, Acupuncture, and Chinese Herbal medicine are widely offered by medical facilities across the United States as complementary or alternative treatments.[31] More health professionals now see the benefits of utilizing a Whole Health approach, and practitioners formulate treatment plans, which focus on meeting the mind, body, and spiritual needs of the whole person.

My purpose here is to bring to light without judgment, the plentiful benefits of certain universal practices proven to integrate the health of mind and body, not to introduce or promote an individual religious or dogmatic tenet of Buddhism, Christianity, Judaism, or any other religion or philosophy. Here, at last, in the *perestroika* of cultural understanding is an opportunity to glean from ancient wisdom that which feeds and prospers our spirit, lest we forget we have one.

Origins of Right Mindfulness

"Do not dwell in the past; do not dream of the future,
Concentrate the mind on the present moment."
~Siddhartha Gautama, the Supreme Buddha

The origins of the practice of right mindfulness and right intention can be found in the teachings of the Buddha. The term Buddha refers to the "enlightened one," or "awakened one."[32] In its simplest form the practice of Right Mindfulness means to practice awareness in all activities of daily life.

The Buddha is not the only one to teach this philosophy. There are many references to right thinking and right mindfulness in other cultures and religions. Like the

Buddha, Jesus instructs his followers in finding the path to peace with self and others through contemplation and prayer, quietness and gentleness of heart.

The Buddha teaches us that through purposeful attention to our speech and actions, the work we honestly engage in throughout our lives will end in peace of heart and mind. He assures us that through the Noble Eightfold Path of

- Right View

- Right Intention

- Right Speech

- Right Action

- Right Livelihood

- Right Effort, and

- Right Mindfulness in daily matters we can attain inner peace.[33] That is, we will experience Universal Harmony and Life Balance as it is meant to be.

Jesus teaches that we must strive to be peacemakers, who are gentle and compassionate to others and to ourselves, especially toward children. He calls on his followers to trust that the mournful will be comforted and those that suffer hardship shall find joy again. His Beatitudes tell us to practice mercy and humility in spirit, and to thirst for justice and righteousness. Jesus promises that in purity of heart we will be blessed so that we may come to experience the kingdom of God, which is within us.[34] Both messages are essentially the same.

Breath...The Sacred Space

"Stress is basically a disconnection from the earth,
a forgetting of the breath. Stress is an ignorant state.
It believes that everything is an emergency.
Nothing is that important, just lie down."
~Natalie Goldberg, American author

The wise men and women from ancient cultures throughout the world, such as Asia, India, Greece, and the Americas, knew the sacred path to present awareness is through the breath. Through attention to and conscious control of our rhythmic breathing we become witness and certifier to every aspect of our lives. Through breath we recognize our true worth, our place in the Universe, and our spiritual and interpersonal connections. It is in the space between the exhalation and inhalation that we understand how we are more than what we seem.

Throughout the history of the North American continent, Native Americans have always known the secret to accessing life peace can be found in a sacred space. To our Native People even the smallest breath can become a personal sanctuary, a place of peace. Mindful breathing is our conscious acknowledgment of the action between the exhalation and the inhalation. One signals the letting go; the other signals renewed life and purpose.

To exhale consciously is to release the negative energy within us, to let go of hurt, pain, misunderstanding, fear, disappointment, embarrassment, judgment, and poor self-worth. More than that, exhaling releases our attachment to joy, happiness, and material things. Only in the letting go can we truly be free to live in inner peace. This is quite a journey by itself.

To inhale consciously is to draw in positive energy in abundance, to restore right mindfulness, love, relationship, empathy, connection and communication with others and ourselves. Right mindfulness combined with its twin, right intention, is the right road to life balance. Breath is the medium on the path.

"To Walk in Balance is to have Heaven (spirituality) and Earth (physicality) in Harmony."[35]

Below is a Lakota Prayer which talks about the power of the sacred space.

> Wakan Tanka, Great Mystery
> Teach me how to trust my heart,
> My mind, my intuition, my inner knowing,
> The senses of my body,
> The blessings of my spirit.
> Teach me to trust these things
> So that I may enter my Sacred Space
> And love beyond my fear
> And thus walk in balance
> With the passing of each glorious sun.[36]

Conclusion

The renowned Buddhist monk, spiritual teacher and peace activist, Thich Nhat Hanh teaches, "By living deeply in the present moment, we can understand the past better and we can prepare for a better future." Amid the chaos and stress of modern life styles there is no longer a need to hold your breath. As you continue forward on your journey to adoption, you now know where to find a much needed rest stop. You now know to begin within.

The practice of mindfulness is your ability to come up for air when you need it, and is a perpetual opportunity to become a better spouse, partner, parent, co-worker, friend, and a better you. Choosing to practice the art of right mindfulness and right intention using conscious breathing is a choice to live fully aware and fully alive. It is a renewable conscious decision to come out of the back of your mind and into your cognitive knowing self. Just breathe!

CHAPTER SIX

TRAFFIC OPTIONS

Parent Training, Education, & Support Groups, Oh My!

"Having children makes you no more a parent than having a piano makes you a pianist."
~Michael Levine

Resource or foster and adoptive parenting is a unique parenting experience. Children adopted internationally and from Child Welfare systems across the United States and around the world face diverse challenges. Experts in this field agree that acquiring new parenting skills and understanding children in new ways are sometimes necessary to facilitate the bonding and attachment process that will lead to family success.[37]

There is much information available from state and private agencies, organizations, and individual professionals to help you understand how traumatic life experiences have impacted your child's development, and what it means to you and your child. But, sorting through it all for the best fit to your family's needs is a daunting task.

The child you have waited for so long does not come without a turbulent history. This only means your eyes should be open and your heart and mind prepared. You will read more about transitions and trauma in the next two chapters. For now, know that a child coming into your home from this situation may be in a state of internal crisis. Without support and specific training, an unsuspecting family is thrown into turmoil all too quickly. Foster and adopted kids come with their trash bags and suitcases full, and I don't mean with clothing. These challenges present unexpected roadblocks to the most seasoned parents. In the event you veer off the road into this ditch, here are three Emergency Road Vehicles to pull you out and set you back on course.

Vehicle One - Resource & Foster Parent Training

Caregivers interested in adopting from the state are required first to become certified Resource or Foster parents. The terminology foster or resource parent is used interchangeably or a single term may be particular to your state. Foster and pre-adoption trainings are offered in every state. In addition to your home inspection and applicable fingerprint and background checks, a mandatory number of training hours must be completed to receive approved resource parent status. The number of hours varies in each state and additional hours of training must be maintained each year your foster home is open.[38]

It is best to check with your state for exact training requirements. Individual training classes range from free to nominal fees per class and are often supplied by the state or an independently contracted training agency. Some state approved courses and trainings are conveniently offered on line. Make certain the ones you take are credited by your state.

Vehicle Two - Parenting Training & Courses

In addition to state requirements, there are also private options for continuing education for pre- and post-adoptive parents. Parents always benefit from fresh skill sets and current information targeted to specific needs in child rearing. As a coach for parents and a parent educator, I offer help and education on the following topics and have seen how parent education enriches the family experience. Seek classes and workshops offered in your area on topics like:

- Understanding childhood trauma
- Facilitating healthy attachment and bonding
- How traumatic events shape a child's life, relationships, and abilities
- Helping children to develop stress coping strategies
- Stress management for special needs caregivers
- Cultural competency in transracial adoptions

Parenting our children is one of the most demanding and critically important responsibilities we share as adults. Yet it is one for which we are least likely to seek sound advice, help, or education. Learning different ways to connect with your child, positively influence behavior, and understand their underlying unmet needs from pre-adoption experiences are your keys to family success. Do not hesitate to seek the help you need early in your adoption experience.

Professionals and parenting coaches like me, who specialize in working with foster, biological, or adoptive families with these special needs, offer an array of excellent alternatives for ongoing family education and accessible support. These additional resources help parents find effective solutions to particular issues they face with their adopted children.

Parent to Parent

As stated earlier, there is a great amount of information out there. By comparison, different courses present conflicting approaches to parenting special needs and fostered or adopted children. Our job as parents is to search for answers that will further the best outcomes for our families. We *do* need to consider our own personal beliefs and parenting styles, as well as the specialized needs of our fostered or adopted children. We *do* need to look at how our past experiences are brought forward in interactions with our children. We *do* need to understand underlying causes of our children's reactions and behaviors in order to help them heal from the trauma of

- Loss of parents
- Multiple foster homes
- Physical abuse
- Emotional neglect
- Fear of Abandonment

Amazingly, many children have survived past traumatic experiences with their resilience intact. Many have not. Our children are not born resilient. Rather, resilience is the outcome of a stable and safe environment with stable and safe caregivers.[39] Implementing an appropriate level of care is important. Finding the best help for your child and family, should you need it, is crucial to your long-term success.

There is wonderful help available. But, you must discern if it is the right help for you and your family. That may take some time. In the *Back Up & Restore* section at the end of this chapter you will find direction in determining what signs you should look for in your child and how you can find help.

Vehicle Three - Parent Support Organizations

There is an abundance of excellent parent support organizations throughout the United States. Yet parents frequently remark to me how difficult it is to find them. Having been in this situation myself, I believe it is not that it is difficult to find a support group. However, it is difficult finding the best one that suits your needs.

Questions to consider in choosing parent support include:

1. What is the group's focus? Some groups focus on particular issues like
- Behaviors
- Autism
- Mental health
- Preventing abuse
- Advocacy and Legal issues
- Adoption and Trauma
- School and IEP (Individualized Education Plan) issues

2. What is the parenting philosophy of the group?
- Tough Love
- Attachment
- Repairing Relationships
- Connection & Responsiveness

3. Does the group address challenges faced by adoptive, grandparent, and kinship caregivers?

4. Does this group offer programs that support through education?
- Are the educational programs supported by current research?
- Are they safe and effective?
- Do they address the needs of the whole child and whole family?
- Do they match with my values and goals?
- Do they support my strengths and needs?

5. What are the group's affiliations?
- Professional organizations and training, which are supported by sound ethics

6. What Certifications, training, and experience do the leaders hold?
- Grief and loss
- Certified in a particular training program such as Non-Violent Communication, Beyond Consequences, or Connection or Attachment Parenting
- Certified Parenting Coach or parent educator
- Conflict Resolution
- Licensed Counselor, Licensed Clinical Therapist, Social Worker, or Nurse
- Other

Conclusion

Savvy parent travelers will anticipate construction delays, detours, and alternate routes. They will prepare by mentally and emotionally figuring in the time it can take to work through this parenting traffic jam and discover new options. Your level of parenting success will increase with your willingness to participate in parent enrichment trainings or courses, educational workshops, and the group support you find among other resource and adoptive parents.

You can never have too much information. You can never have too much support. You need only time and help to shovel the gravel from under your tires and get the traction you need to continue on. Seize the day!

Back Up & Restore

Spotlighting Children's Mental Health

Empowering Families from the Inside Out

The U.S. Surgeon General's Conference Report on Children's Mental Health in 2000 implied that we were facing a public crisis in mental health care for all children, from infants through adolescents. The Report stated at that time, "Evidence compiled by the World Health Organization indicates that by the year 2020, childhood neuropsychiatric disorders will rise proportionately by over 50 percent, internationally, to become one of the five most common causes of morbidity, mortality, and disability among children."[40]

In the light of these harsh facts it is crucial parents understand how early mental health prevention and intervention for children, and accessible supportive community services for parents, helps secure long-term stability and future success of families.

Although the above statistics are more than a decade old, they hold strong relevance today. Despite challenges and positive changes in our nation's mental health systems of care, significant numbers of families enter into crisis each year as a result of increasing mental health diagnoses in children and adolescents. That amounts to approximately 20% of American children.[41] Children are being diagnosed with mental illnesses at younger ages and at alarming rates. How can parents and caregivers be prepared?

Know If Your Child Is at Risk

Children who have experienced traumatic situations or losses early in life, whether a single incident or over prolonged periods are at significant risk for developing mental and emotional health disorders due to over-whelming inability to cope with the underlying stress.[42] A list of the causes of potential traumatic effects on children and adults is warranted here and can include the following:

- Abuse (physical and sexual)
- Neglect and abandonment
- Pre and post-natal trauma (difficult or compli-cated birth)
- Pre-natal exposure to drugs and alcohol
- Adoption (foreign and domestic)
- Institutional Care (Orphanage or Residential Treatment Center)
- Medical trauma (painful medical procedures and long hospitalizations)
- Prolonged illness (personal or someone close to us)
- Trauma from accidents (falls from bikes, falls down stairs, automobile, other)
- Animal attacks
- Foster Care or multiple disruptions of care
- Unstable or unsafe environment
- Loss of caregiver or many caregivers due to foster care, violence, or death
- A witness to or victim of random violence or domestic violence
- A victim of bullying
- Divorce or separation from primary caregiver
- Natural Disasters and war[43]

Know the Signs

- Seeming inability to self-soothe or regulate emotion
- Prolonged sleeping difficulties
- Prolonged eating difficulties
- Intense fears which do not go away
- Bedwetting
- Poor or fleeting eye contact
- Intense or unusual behavioral displays or outbursts
- Tendency to withdraw from playmates or social situations
- Self-harm or thoughts of death
- Intense anger, defiance or aggression
- Sudden drop in grades, social isolation or school aversion
- Risk taking such as in sexual behaviors, use of drugs, alcohol, and other substance abuse
- Sudden changes in moods or hypo/hyperactivity

Know How to Get Help

If you have a nagging question about certain behaviors, trust your gut.

- If your child is a foster child, contact their case worker or supervisor to discuss your concerns and how best to proceed
- Contact your child's pediatrician or primary care doctor for possible screening, assessments, and referrals
- Do not quit asking until you get the answers you need to help your child

- Do not rely on information from the Internet to self-diagnose your child, it will only increase your fear and you might incorrectly apply symptoms to your child

- If your child has a diagnosis, DO consult the DSM IV (Diagnostic and Statistical Manual of Mental Disorders) online to better understand possible implications of the diagnosis, and DO ask your doctor or mental health professional to help you interpret what you read

- Develop a sound home and community action plan for the safety of your family and child; know who to call and when

- Identify supportive resources within family and community, which may include church, parenting coach, and healthcare professional or local hospital crisis center

- Find educational opportunities through classes and workshops, which offer training to better understand your child's difficulties and build and enrich new parenting skills.

- Remember you are never alone in your struggle to raise your child. Search for ways to connect with others who share your experience through online and local support groups.

Know the Facts

"One of every ten children and adolescents suffers from mental illness in the United States."[44] This means one in ten families is in crisis. Children and families in crisis mean higher risk for:

- Depression
- Child neglect or abuse

- Spouse/partner abuse
- Marital problems, separation, or divorce
- Eating disorders
- Increased physical illness in parents due to prolonged elevated stress
- Secondary traumatic stress in siblings and other family members living with and caring for high-risk children
- Disintegration of relationships within families
- Isolation in the community, suicide

Early care, intervention, and education for families lead to improved outcomes for children at risk to develop mental illness. Early recognition of childhood emotional difficulties leads to the development of stronger support systems for parents and caregivers. A well-integrated mental health care plan for children and accessible supportive community services for parents helps secure the stability and future success of our families.

When parents are educated and supported in the best care options for their children, families become empowered from the inside out. An empowered family is a strong and sustainable family! And this is the desired outcome we all want!

CHAPTER   SEVEN

INTERSECTIONS

Lessons in Transition, Trust & Love

Transitions, trust, and feeling secure and loved are issues that children adopted privately or from the foster care system struggle with into adulthood. What will happen when your lives intersect? The foundation of your parent-child relationship will strengthen according to your knowledge of how these issues affect your child. In my personal experience, approaching issues involving transition, trust, and emotional security with sensitivity, empathy, and right information will make all the difference in your new relationship with your child.

> *"Home...hard to know what it is if you've never had one.*
> *Home...I can't say where it is but I know I'm going home*
> *That's where the hurt is."*
>
> ~U2

Transitions - Transition means a passage from one form, state, style, or place to another. For our children, regardless of age, this meant a single move away from the birth parent, or multiple moves from one home to another many times. The moves resulted in loss of toys, a familiar bed, changes in caregivers, parents, siblings, and that special smell of a bedtime toy.

One parent tells the story of her young child's journey this way: "My child was left in the hospital two days after his birth. He remained in the NICU for 10 days before being placed in his temporary first home. By the time he came to me at 9 months he had already been in four placements. He would cry and cling to me whenever he saw someone he didn't know. He needed a lot of special care to feel secure and know he wasn't going to leave us."

Another parent relates her transition story: "My daughter came to us when she was 8 years old. Her history stated she had been in six foster placements prior to coming to us. If she misbehaved in some way, she would go and stand at the door with her coat expecting to leave. When I realized what she had gone through, I understood why she was afraid to trust us. She couldn't know what forever or permanent meant."

It is clear that the physical and emotional disruptions our kids experience at their tender ages would be difficult for most adults to endure. Moreover, what has happened to them, from their perspective, happened against their will and beyond their control. It was taken out of their hands. These experiences shape their understanding of life, home, family, and relationships. What can you do to ease the process of transitioning your child into a permanent home? What do you need to understand?

Establishing trust between you and your child goes a long way to heal past hurts. But don't expect it to happen overnight. Remember, each time your child was moved in the system, he or she left behind bits and pieces of their life, belongings, family, heritage, language, and culture. Our children have experienced relationship and family as broken and painful at young, tender ages. This type of loss is a deep hurt that heals very slowly. But, you CAN heal it.

Children need to know they will be safe in this new place they will call home. They need to know and trust that they can feel safe and be safe with *you*. This may be a brand new feeling for them as safe may not be in their emotional memory. They will only learn it if you model it for them again, and again, and again. When they begin to feel safe with you, they will begin to trust you.

Will you be the parent who shows this child what it means to have a parents' limitless love for him or her? Limitless and uncommon love is to give without judgment or pre-qualification. Your child learns to see his or her value mirrored in your eyes and in your words, and they may not be able to accept it at first. In fact, your child may reject it outright. Please do not allow this to deter you from loving and committing to this hurt child, whose experience has left them with the only belief they can have about their self: "I am not loved. I am not worth loving. I can never believe anyone would ever really love me."

As a parent, your love, limits, and tolerance will be tested. Traditionally, we have come to believe that when a child pushes our limits, we should respond with strict punishments. If this is your course now, your actions may delay the critical period of development of trust and attachment between you and your child. You must consistently show a living illustration of what it looks like to have a loving, healthy relationship between a parent and child. Never presume your child remembers how much you love him, or that you told him yesterday or this morning. As absurd as it sounds, you may have to prove you love your child with each opportunity that presents itself until their wounded heart begins to remember.

Your patience and uncompromising dedication changes their belief that they are not worth loving and makes real the bond between you. Then the heart of your child will open and painful cracks left by past, hurtful experiences will begin to fill. Love never has to be perfect; it does have to be ever present.

Trust - Children do well when they trust that the adults who care for them will consistently nurture all of their needs. What do children need?

- Food and nutrition to establish good health in mind and body
- Warmth on all levels of the material, physical, and emotional
- Physical touch through hugs and tender affection from caregiver
- Responsive care and predictability...that is, knowing the adult will provide and take care of them in a timely manner
- Love, security and uncompromised connections with other human beings who are consistently in their lives
- Boundaries, structure, and limits with respect and understanding in order to create an environment of safety, learning, physical and spiritual growth
- Joy, play and laughter within any opportunities for optimal bonding and attachment to occur with a primary caregiver

Trust happens when the caregiver meets the child's needs well enough and often enough. Simply meeting the need is not sufficient. What is critical is the caregiver's empathic approach with the child in order to fill his need. As trust develops, so does love, dependency, and attachment.

This passage from the well-loved *Winnie the Pooh* series sums up the needs for trust of all children.

> *Piglet sidled up to Pooh from behind.*
> *"Pooh!" He whispered.*
> *"Yes, Piglet?"*
> *"Nothing," said Piglet, taking Pooh's paw.*
> *"I just wanted to be sure of you."*
>
> ~A.A. Milne

Love - Kids think in concrete terms. Life situations are black and white, soft and hard, and light and dark. Children can experience the receipt of love as a condition of parental care. They learn to believe the fulfillment of their need for nurturing attention is contingent upon their ability to *earn* it.[45]

For instance, a foster child having been moved many times to different homes and longing in her heart for permanency in her current placement may reason: "I must be bad for this to happen." (That is, losing parents and multiple placements) Therefore, "If I can make myself good, perhaps I can live here." "If I do whatever they want, maybe *these* parents will really love and care about me. Maybe this time I won't have to leave here and be sent to a different family." She already perceives her worth to be in default. She concludes she must be bad for these bad things to have happened to her. She too willingly takes on personal responsibility to try and *earn* the love and devotion of her new caregivers. She plans to prove she is worthy of their love.

Children coming from foster care or out-of-home placement into adoption frequently have not had the consistency of relationship with sensitive caregivers which provides them the vital support necessary to interpret the traumatic losses and confusing experiences they have suffered. Some of these children will need time and extra support to feel safe again and integrate these traumatic events into their daily lives. Internal belief systems that have been conditioned to tell them they are bad or good, worthy or worthless, capable or incapable, intelligent or stupid, lovable or unlovable, are too often unintentionally reinforced by the conditional expectations of the adults in their lives. Children in foster care and adoptive circumstances are too familiar with conditional love. The love you give your child will have to be different. It will have to be an uncommon love.

Alternately, children may display destructive behaviors in an attempt to self-protect and reduce emotional pain.[46] Prior experience may cause them to work toward preventing what they long for the most...your love. While we have come to believe that some children *consciously* construct negative situations to protect themselves from further emotional pain, recent advances in neuroscience and brain development proves the contrary. Kids with emotional pain act out from an *unconscious* place of primitive self-survival.[47]

Parents of children who have suffered early traumatic loss need to reexamine their former parenting beliefs and practices, as they may no longer be valid in the face of their foster and adopted child's experiences. When children experience life as hurtful, painful, and frightening, they will expect these outcomes to be true always. It is important to know that what we believe becomes the framework for our personal reality.[48]

Perception is everything. Some of the reactions governing this child's behaviors stem from deeply imprinted belief systems. The parent or caregiver of a child or youth in this state of belief can anticipate and predict certain behavioral responses by the child to his or her environment and those around them according to this pre-established framework. This is the structural belief system from which the child's body and mind now operate. This is how they view life. An explanation of the development of sensory and emotional memory, and how it drives certain behaviors in children, further illustrates the body and brain framework of the foster and adopted child.

Origins of Sensory & Emotional Memory

Our brains are use dependent. If we don't use it, we do lose it. Moreover, information stored in our brains is dependent upon what we experience. Brains are the sum result and miracle of humanity's developmental progress. They store experiential information at the sensory and emotional level. The brain processes the information through a complex series of neuronal connections and later synapses. These neuronal formations begin to develop approximately 42 days after gestation. All we know in life begins as a sensory experience. As we grow and interact with the world around us, our brain plays an intricate match game with sights, sounds, sensations, and emotions. In the first three years of life our brains will assign billions of stored sensory memories to particular life experiences. Sensory and emotional input, and its critical organization in our brains, lays the foundation for how we ultimately understand and relate to life and the world around us.

The foundations of sensory and emotional memory development particularly, provide clues to foster and adopted kids' behaviors. You already have knowledge about the general experience of adopted children coming out of the Child Welfare systems, orphanages, or other out-of-home placements, and these are disruptions of the child's lifeline. We might say the disrupted foster or adopted child's emotional and relational experience is like repeatedly trying to start a car on a cold winter day, and each time the engine starts to warm up a sudden blast of frigid temperatures abruptly forces it to shut down.

The physical disruptions contribute to emotional and sensory disruptions in the child's ongoing development. Thus, the child experiences his or her emotions and relationships through a series of false starts and abrupt stops. When the time finally arrives for the child to have a permanent home with loving parents the child's emotions are in semi-permanent shut down. Imagine the emotional struggle and time it takes for a foster child, of any age, to become accustomed to the people and rules of a new household, understand how unfamiliar caregivers and foster siblings might act toward them, and how they themselves are accepted in return. Imagine that as the child eventually gains enough trust to feel close to the family they are with, then to have the placement disrupted and the child placed in yet another foreign and uncertain situation. When this occurs the child's emotions, the lifelines that lead them to connections, attachments, and trust with others, learn to shut down.

The child's emotional and sensory systems become fixed in the belief that to self-protect is the only safety they can count on. Recognizing your child comes to you in this state of emotional disconnect is a key to understanding your child's emotional needs as it gives you vital clues to understand and manage their behavioral responses.

The following story about baby Eleanora gives you a glimpse into one couple's early foster-adoption experience in learning how to interpret their young child's delayed emotional and sensory development. Can you find the clues to the reasons behind baby Eleanora's behaviors?

Baby Eleanora

Charlotte and George were thrilled with the placement of a ten-month old cutie pie whom they call Eleanora. Eleanora was placed as a foster child with George and Charlotte, and together the hopeful couple and baby made their way toward their future adoption day. George and Charlotte were Eleanora's third foster placement and they were attentive and loving foster parents to baby Eleanora. They cooed and fussed over her with all the excitement of new parents and bonded with the baby immediately. Eleanora seemed cool toward their affectionate displays and George and Charlotte concluded that the baby needed time to warm up to them. Eleanora's caseworker told the couple that the baby was babbling and her vocabulary consisted of a few words. During the first weeks they noticed that Eleanora was not trying to say words or mimic sounds. Although this was a concern to Charlotte and George, they believed the child was just being shy with them.

Charlotte and her husband viewed Eleanora as the perfect baby. She appeared to have an easy temperament, was not demanding, and seemed content in her new home. Throughout the early weeks, Eleanora gained weight and appeared to progress well. Yet Charlotte felt it was frequently difficult for her to read little Eleanora's needs, and the baby was inconsistent in the manner she responded to particular situations. For instance, the couple had a large family and many friends who frequently came to their home to visit with them and their new foster child, as there was a flurry of excitement over the baby's arrival. Charlotte noticed that the baby's body would stiffen when others would hold her, and she remained aloof. The baby would turn her face away from those trying to interact with her and become overly quiet in social or family gatherings.

Eleanora's eyes would grow wide and she appeared hyper-vigilant to her surroundings. During these encounters with others, baby Eleanora became extremely clingy with her foster mom, and Charlotte was unable to leave the child or put her down without the baby's inevitable prolonged and distressed crying.

Eleanora was also having trouble sleeping through the night. Charlotte sometimes found it quite difficult to soothe and comfort the baby in her distress, and this was a source of stress for both parents. Alternately, Charlotte saw a completely different response from Eleanora when only one or two family members came to visit. In this instance, Eleanora became somewhat responsive to the family members, and although very reserved and cautious, was more apt to smile and play with them. Charlotte always felt it was a guessing game to discover what the babies' signals meant.

Evaluating Baby Eleanora's Behaviors

Even with the minimal history we know about baby Eleanora, we begin to piece together the meaning behind the behaviors she displays and discuss solutions to help George and Charlotte meet their daughter's needs. We see that the two previous disruptions in placement in early infancy, which is a critical time in child development and attachment, have interrupted Eleanora's development in several ways. Were you able to identify the ways as you read the story? Were you able to connect how early breaks and inconsistency in caregivers upset the foundation for Eleanora's emotional security? If not, reread the story to attempt to pick out the clues. They are also listed below.

  • Eleanora's cool demeanor in response to her foster parent's affection is indicative of the lingering effects of earlier breaks in the bonding process. (These are the emotional false starts and abrupt stops we spoke about in the analogy of the cold car engine).

• Eleanora is a ten-month old baby girl who comes to her foster parents with reports that she is babbling, speaking words, and meeting her developmental milestones. This is a sign that Eleanora adjusted well in her last placement and was thriving and progressing normally. The physical disruption to her emotional security because of the new placement has caused a regression in speech development, and Eleanora's speech is now slightly delayed.

• Eleanora's sleep is disturbed, and she is not sleeping through the night. The child cannot yet feel safe with different foster parents, in a different crib, in a different room, in a different house. Nothing is familiar and the baby's system cannot settle down enough to allow her to remain asleep.

• Eleanora is clearly uncomfortable with persons she is not familiar with, and shows it by stiffening her body (an unconscious fear response to her stressful situation).

• Eleanora is overwhelmed in new situations and her brain automatically directs her body to self-protect. She turns her face away from the surrounding activity and people in an attempt to decrease sensory stimulation and her internal state of stress.

• Eleanora has stored upsetting emotional memories related to being taken away from her prior caregivers and other negative experiences associated with her prior displacements. Although she is not yet talking, her brain relates each experience to an available emotional memory. In this example, Eleanora's current experiences, although they are positive, are connected to past negative emotional memories. In the above example we see fear and insecurity triggered in Eleanora when she is with unfamiliar people, even though they are gentle and loving with her, and she manifests her fear by a wide-eyed look and hyper-vigilance to her surroundings. She shows her intense feelings of insecurity, fear, and vulnerability in her interrupted sleep patterns by clinging desperately to her foster mother, and she displays inconsolable distress when they must separate.

Knowing more details about the circumstances of Eleanora's prior placements and how she entered the foster care system will assist George and Charlotte to provide the best care for their new foster child.

Eleanora's Placement History

George and Charlotte are problem solvers and are devoted to finding answers that will help them understand baby Eleanora's behaviors. They first call the caseworker to ask if she can shed light on what they are experiencing with their baby. Perhaps the caseworker has additional information, which will help them understand their baby's past, so they can make better choices for her now. The couple is equally concerned about the baby's lack of babbling. Their caseworker suggests the couple contact a neurologist for answers to Eleanora's speech delays, and to rule out more serious matters.

The caseworker is supportive, and is able to give the concerned couple minimal information on the baby's background. She informs the couple that the baby went home with her natural mother after birth, and came into the system as the result of substantiated reports of abuse to other children in the home. As a result, all the children were removed from the home. The baby was then 3 months old. She spent three days in the hospital for dehydration and was placed in her first foster home where she remained until she was 5 months old. Eleanora was removed from this placement due to unforeseen illness of an extended family member to the foster family. Next, the baby was placed with an older couple where she remained until she was removed at 10 months and placed with George and Charlotte. The information given by the caseworker helps George and Charlotte to better understand their baby's disrupted history of caregivers, and they are forming a clearer image of how these things have affected her.

George and Charlotte then turn to a nearby professional coach for parents to help them formulate a plan to address Eleanora's emotional needs. Over the following three months they explore the differences in typical development and Eleanora's disrupted development, and the couple learns how they can facilitate healing through little Eleanora's attachment and bond with them.

As a team they formulate a goal for sensitive parenting to help Eleanora regain her sense of security with Charlotte and George, and implement strategies for meeting their child's needs on a deeper level of care. The list below contains a few of the strategies the informed pre-adoptive parents put in place to help their child flourish under their care.

- George and Charlotte will provide their young daughter whatever time she needs to adjust in her new environment. To this end, they will limit visitors to their home to individuals or very small groups, and for less frequent and time-limited visits, until Eleanora shows advances in her comfort level being with strangers. George and Charlotte will know she is ready to advance to being in larger groups, when the baby responds with easy smiles, and displays enjoyment at being with extended family members or friends.

· George and Charlotte will maintain a calm, quiet, and soothing atmosphere in their home to calm any distress Eleanora may be experiencing in her new surroundings. This may include soft instrumental music before naptime and bedtime, and upon waking and returning home. A music box, or stuffed animal with a music box inside, played at similar times to those listed above will also assist the baby to connect the good feelings of coming home, or the comfort of sleep, associated with hearing the music. Loud noises like; slamming doors, shouting, yelling, or other angry sounding voices, and loud or prolonged radio and tele-vision with raised volume, will be kept to a minimum for the first three months. This will allow the baby's frightened and distressed regulatory system to settle back into a calm state natural to the child's internal systems. More time might be required to help the child re-regulate internally, and will be assessed as the child progresses.

· The pre-adoptive parents will temporarily limit the outings they have with Eleanora, as these produce the same emotional upset the baby is exposed to in large groups when at home. With their mindful observation of the baby's progress, they will then slowly reintro-duce Eleanora to a more active social life.

· George and Charlotte recognize that their baby has not had the benefits of safe and consistent emotional and physical caregiving afforded to other children her age. They will counter the baby's early neglect and insecurity, by providing her with more attuned parenting. They will carry Eleanora on tour throughout the house regularly, and show Eleanora around each room, so she will become familiar with where she is. The couple is encouraged to hide toys in the rooms and encourage Eleanora to explore and find them. This activity will supply Eleanora with positive and happy experiences in each room of the house with her new parents.

- Charlotte and George will provide relationship rich opportunities for Eleanora to regain internal security, by keeping in close proximity to the baby as much as is possible. Their coach's suggestion leads the couple to move Eleanora's crib into their bedroom for temporary co-sleeping, so the baby will have the comfort of hearing their breathing, and seeing their presence when she wakes at night.

- Their parenting coach also instructs the couple to carry Eleanora in a baby sling which has the child snuggled next to them. The coach wants Eleanora to associate the warmth, soothing voices, and smell of her parents, with her increasing emotional safety.

Within a few months the family saw success as a result of their efforts to help their new child transition to a new environment. By the time Eleanora reached the 19-months mark, she was sleeping in her own room, saying simple sentences, going to play dates, and blowing kisses to charmed visitors and family. The above strategies support and enrich the secure relationship, which parents and child are building together. Their sensitive and enlightened caregiving now allows for a deeper appreciation of the issues and reasons behind a child's behaviors, and what might be done to effect healing and change.

Since you now recognize that your foster child experiences emotional disconnection, you can predict reasons for and how a child might respond in certain situations. You'll observe what triggers the responses and the belief related to it. You will also learn how to help them change their perceptions.

Some children achieve a radical change in their belief systems as easily as a sensitive caregiver bringing them into a safe home environment, giving them enough good food, and showing them that parents can love, care, be kind, protective, and attentive to the needs of their children. Not all of your experiences with your children will be this easy. Altering pre-conditioned perceptions for any adult, child, or us is akin to hacking out a new trail through the thickest jungle. The journey takes time and sweat equity, but it's worth it.

The Function of Behavior as Communication

Developing a secure child-parent relationship through the nurturing principles of uncompromising love and trust, you will view all behavior, whether positive or negative, as your child's earnest attempt to communicate how they feel inside. Yet, that you understand what is going on within your child is not enough. Your child must know you understand him from a deeper level than what he shows you on the surface.

Here are ten directional markers to show you how all behavior is communication. These ten markers and their subsequent explanations also utilize the principles of effective communication you learned in Chapter Five, and will help you apply them in your relationship with your child.

Ten Directional Markers to Navigate Behavioral Communication

The following navigation tools are bolded and include examples and scenarios to illustrate and synthesize what has been discussed in this chapter.

1. Observe behavior to decode possible meaning and underlying causes or triggers related to the behavior.
There is meaning and cause behind every positive or negative reaction. I frequently speak to parents about the need to view their child's behavior as if they were detectives looking for clues to solve a mystery. This involves thinking on your feet and being mindful and attentive to your child's emotions and feelings. It also involves being aware that things are not always as they seem. The behavioral clues we look for (or decode) to tell us why our children may be acting as they do, or what need our child has that has to be met, will not always be in plain sight.

Furthermore, your foster or adopted child's most urgent needs may be masked by opposite emotions, words, behaviors and attitudes which can be misinterpreted by the caregiver. For example, when you are trying to the best of your ability to show love, care, and respect to your 9-year-old foster child, and they respond with a defiant attitude and refuse your affection, you will remember that this child's life experiences have made him fearful and distrusting of close relationships. They will continue to push you away until your consistent uncommon loving approach creates trust and changes their belief. You must consider that what you see on the surface of this child is the opposite of what they most want and need from you.

A child's demeanor may exhibit anywhere on the

behavioral scale from extreme withdrawal or shutdown, self-isolation, fleeting eye contact, or dissociation of feelings to being obstinate, defensive, defiant, or explosive. To decode the meaning of your child's behavior, focus on what the behavior is telling you *about* your child. You must learn how to read and decode your child's behavior, and below is a story that shows how one parent did it.

An adoptive dad explained his experience with his pre-teen daughter this way.

"My daughter had a difficult time adjusting to living with us after her placement. I used to refer to her as a child trapped inside herself. I could sometimes see how much she wanted to play and just be a happy kid, but I could also see the intensity of her anger, fear, and internal conflict. It afflicted everyone around her, and it seemed as though she did everything she could to keep us at arm's length."

"At first we couldn't understand why she acted this way; why she was so defensive. With help and support, we were able to understand the basis for her behavior, and help her work through grief and intense anger over having been removed by the state from her birth family. Because it took place when she was young, she had a confused memory of what really happened. There was even a period of time she blamed my wife and I, as if we were the ones who physically took her away from them. It hurts to know how much internal pain and confusion she felt about her past and how deeply it affected her. When she began to trust us, she was able to share her pain and past hurts. Only then did I feel our family begin to grow. Now we are well on our way to healing. It took all of us together to make it happen."

In my spare time I enjoy watching television episodes about storm chasers. This gives me another way to explain decoding. Decoding behavior is like looking at a rain wrapped tornado crossing the road in front of you. You see the fury of rain, hail, wind and debris, but you have to look real hard to see the driving force behind it. Whether you are raising or working with children, this is exactly the skill you need to develop to be the best parent, caregiver, and healer to your child.

2. Understand that patterns of strong behavioral reactions in children with disrupted and high stress histories are rooted in past fearful experiences, and are easily triggered by simple changes or transitions in everyday life.

Just as we store pleasant memories connected to good feelings and emotions, we also store frightening, stressful memories connected to fearful and confusing feelings. Neuroscience tells us that we have easy recall of positive emotional memories, which strengthen our inner resources and allow for their easy access. However, fear-triggering emotional memories embed at a deeper level in the brain and trigger primitive survival reactions known as fight, flight, and freeze. Next, the child goes into a state of overwhelm that undermines his ability to access resilience or other internal resources. The well-worn neural pathways these negative emotional memories travel in the brains and bodies of children create higher levels of stress, which ignites the perception that something is happening to them which might present life-threatening danger, and thus resulting are predictable patterns of behavior. Parents can expect to see these patterns of behavior emerging around every-day transitional events, such as:

- Change in, addition to, or interruption in daily schedule

- Leaving for school or day care (especially after weekend or holiday breaks)

- Returning from school or day care

- Riding a school bus in between home and school
- Changing class rooms or activities in school or at home (even when these activities are perceived by the parent or teacher to be fun and enjoyable)
- Leaving home for any activity like going to a supermarket, play park, shopping, etc.
- After arriving at a destination, your child may not be able to leave the car
- At events or social activities, your child may shadow you and refuse to break away to enjoy the festivities, or your child may become hyperactive, overly silly, and find it difficult or impossible to regulate their emotional self or their actions
- Leaving for and returning from parental visitation may be intensely difficult for some foster children placed in a pre-adoptive home

When Leaving Doesn't Mean Coming Back

Children in foster care have experienced being taken away in a variety of life shattering and frightening circumstances. Removing a child from their home and natural parents is a shocking, distressing, and sometimes aggressive act for the child to witness and experience. Police and CPS personnel may enter the home and take a child by force. No parent *wants* to give up his or her child. The child may have witnessed their parent being restrained amid yelling and screaming.

Although child protective workers take measures to alleviate trauma surrounding removal of children from their homes wherever and whenever possible, this cannot always be accomplished due to immediate safety concerns for the child or children being removed. Many times being taken away meant that it was done by complete strangers to the child, and involved never returning to the same location or seeing the same persons again, whether this was their family of origin, the school the child attended, or the homes they lived in. A caseworker may have arrived unexpectedly to take the child from school to a new foster home, without giving the child the opportunity to say goodbye to their caregivers or foster siblings, or without gathering personal items to take with them. They may have been removed from a home late at night; perhaps as they were preparing for bed, because this was when the caseworker was available. They were taken to a new home at a time when they were supposed to be falling asleep in a familiar place where they felt safe.

The new place only increased the fear, confusion, insecurity, and uncertainty of life. Now they were with strangers who didn't know them at all. Perhaps they were lied to when they were told they were going on vacation but never returned to their former foster home. If your child has come from an orphanage situation, it is likely all their caregivers were called *mommy*, and your child's emotional memory states that *mommy* is synonymous with something exchangeable and impermanent. Therefore, although the child remained in one place, the caregivers or *mommies* were always different.

Applying the above information to understanding your child and behaviors it is easier to see that the fear the child experiences now or the turmoil they may create surrounding your suggestion of a fun trip to the park makes perfect sense once you see the bigger picture from the child's perspective. You may look at the child's placement with you as permanent. They do not. Not yet. You are just another stranger, and your child will not know where you are really taking him or her, or if they will ever return.

Prospective foster and adoptive parents do not have to worry that these more severe behavioral patterns will become evident in every child from foster care. Parents and caregivers benefit from this knowledge to be able to recognize that some children will be more dramatically affected by early traumatic life experiences and they may need additional emotional and psychological support. As parents you will become vigilant to these patterns and will eventually be able to determine what they mean, and with training, how you can help.

Behavioral Patterns Triggered by Daily Life

Let us examine the following scenario that illustrates the above information.

Scenario I - An adoptive mother notices that whenever she leaves her daughter for any reason, her daughter displays a variety of confusing, highly reactive, or sometimes negative behaviors, as you will see described in the examples below. Over time the mother sees a pattern in her daughter's reactive behaviors. What are the clues to decoding this child's behavioral response?

The mother first looks at the behavior to understand what is prompting it. The mother also wisely recognizes that there is some connection between her leaving and the rise in behaviors she witnesses. This scenario provides a few examples:

It's time for mother to leave for work. Her 8-year-old daughter initially is clingy and desperately shadows parent around the house, as parent gets ready for work. After a period of anxious begging and pleading for parent to remain home, the daughter becomes aggravated and angry with her parent. The daughter becomes insolent and insults her parent, even spits on or rejects parent's offered comfort, and her attempt to explain why she must leave. The daughter refuses the parent's touch and ignores parent when she leaves. Daughter screams, "I will never love you!" as parent closes the door.

The above example, although unsettling for the parent, is simple to decode with a little curiosity and mindful attunement by the parent. One can presume from the child's foster and adoptive history that this child is reacting to the trigger of her adoptive mother leaving from her deep-seated fear of abandonment. We then see this child's internal alarms sounding signals that she should fight to gain control in what the child experiences as an uncontrollable and possibly horrifying situation. Each action the child displays is an unconscious and desperate effort to regain her lost security and not a pre-planned and well-executed rebellion against the parent or caregiver.

What happens when the signals given by your child are more obscure, as is sometimes the case?

Scenario 2 - It's time for dad to leave for work. He becomes aware of his two adopted children fighting in the living room. It slowly escalates. He hears his older child, a ten-year old boy (who was abused as a toddler, and the target child in this scenario) making high-pitched screechy sounds, followed by some form of hyper-activity, such as; deliberately banging into furniture, knocking items over, falling on the floor, or jumping on the couch. The boy throws a sofa pillow across the room at his sister, goading the younger child into a fight. Insults come in the form of breathless whispers from the boy aimed at his younger sister. Suddenly the ten-year old boy leaves the living room and enters his bedroom. He tears up the room, kicking his closet doors, pulling dresser drawers out and scattering clothing and personal items, yelling all the while how he hates his life and wishes he were dead. When dad tries to strictly intervene and stop the commotion, his hyper-aroused son turns his fury against the parent in a physical altercation.

Renowned child trauma specialist, Dr. Bruce Perry, cautions that maltreated children who have suffered familial abuse and are in a persistent state of hyper-arousal will react anxiously or aggressively to illicit a similar aggressive response from their caregiver in order to have control over what is happening to them in their environment, since they had no control over what happened against them in prior circumstances. Dr. Perry goes on to say that the highly adaptive survival skills the child automatically developed in their earlier situations are now being called up and utilized in a maladaptive way, as self-survival defenses against what is perceived by the child as threatening interactions with foster and adoptive parents, teachers, or siblings. In a paper titled, *Incubated in Terror: Neurodevelopmental Factors in the 'Cycle of Violence*, Dr. Perry writes, "This behavior is often misinterpreted and the school or foster placement will punish them (the child) severely (often after a restraint situation) and reinforce the child's view of the world – adults are aggressive and solve problems using force. Our ineffective child protective, mental health and juvenile justice systems teach this lesson to children again and again — until they are big enough, smart enough or violent enough to turn the tables."[49] We must change and humanize our treatment approach to traumatized children and youth.

On the surface, the hyper reactivity the ten-year old boy displays in the scenario appears unrelated to the dad's actions of leaving for work. Parents report seeing behaviors, which appear as, not related to the event. This makes it difficult for parents to relate the behavioral display back to its cause or trigger. This is where you must understand the relationship between the cause and its effect.

In this real life example, the child's strong negative behavioral response relates to his sense of abandonment and triggered fear that his dad will not return. The abandonment ignites the child's internal belief that the parent does not love or care for him, which is the child's perception of why the parent is leaving, and the boy lashes out at the nearby sibling and ultimately at himself. This child has an intense internal fear of being left alone and holds internal grief related to his loss that becomes severe separation anxiety with the parent. Parents also see this response when the child has to leave the parent, such as for school. While on the surface this behavior is disturbing and disrupting, it is also a positive sign: this child is developing an attachment toward their parent, and is desperately fearful of anything that might threaten the relationship. This fear creates a heightened state of stress in the body. Fear and stress are directly related and centered in the part of the brain that governs our survival reactions. A direct result of the electrical impulses fired off within the brain, because of the environmental fears or stressors, results in the child's behavior. To say this child is scared to death, and they will react in such a way as to save their life at all costs, is the truth.[50]

We understand this process better if we view the previous scenario as an example of released energy.

- The cause or trigger is the parent leaving the child, which produces a fear reaction in the brain and body (fear, anxiety, and stress). This initiates a powerful chemical release of life-saving energy in the brain that travels throughout the body and is manifest in the actions and resulting behaviors of the child. The child's brain perceives the environment as threatening.

- Negative impulses will lead to an external physical or emotional reaction and look like anger, crying, hiding, fighting with a sibling, stomping feet, cursing, throwing objects, breaking toys, spitting, running to the child's room, or running away. Although this is not the desired behavior we hope to see in a child, we recognize the powerful control emotional impulses exert on a child's psyche, and the child's inability to regain emotional balance.

- We now recognize the child's requirement for external support in the safe expression of their internal explosive emotions. The child's emotionally compromised internal state is now dependent upon the emotionally regulated, external and internal state of the adult caregiver. If the *calm and deliberately well-regulated guidance and support from involved adults* is not available, or if the child is forcefully prevented from expressing their emotional upset, the negative emotional energy buries deep in the body mind system compounding earlier trauma, anxiety, and stress.

These processes occur normally yet at a lesser intensity all the time. They are automatic, imperceptible to us, and are the sole cause for most of our reactions governing self-preservation and survival.

Following the principle that the way in which we approach the child is critical, here are viable suggestions, which will assist you and your child in the development of appropriate coping skills and the building of a sensitive and trusting relationship.

3. State your observation on the situation without blame or judgment.

Example: "I noticed you get very upset whenever I have to leave you and go to work, honey. I know you are afraid I may not come back home because that is what happened to you before, but I will always come back home to you." You may give the child permission to contact you during your time away from each other, or you will connect with them. This will reassure them you are completing whatever errand you set out to do, and that you are indeed returning.

4. Become familiar and comfortable with identifying and parenting your child's emotional age.

When traumatic stress impacts children, any regressive behavior is more pronounced. Children of any chronological age become whiney and act younger when they feel stress and fear increase. Your teen may tantrum like a two year old, a toddler may revert to soiling after potty training, or a pre-teen may speak baby talk. This regressive behavior is a signal your child is in need of your care and attention.

It is important you meet your child's emotional need and relate to your child at their emotional level. Relating regressive behaviors to our example, we view the child's underlying need as an authentic need to be cuddled and snuggled, nurtured tenderly and reassured. This may be exactly what they need whether they are five or fifteen. In the face of being without you, your child is feeling uncertain about his immediate welfare. His behavior will be the measure of his vulnerability. This reaction would not be uncommon behavior in foster children. As the parent, your challenge is to believe them, to not think of them as devious or manipulative. Your ultimate goal is to empathize, reassure, soothe, allow and support their emotional process (through their expression of crying or safely displaying of anger, etc.), and bring them back into safety again.

5. Create safety. Reassure your child they are all right and that you will remain with them until they feel safe again.

Example: "We miss each other so much when we are apart. How about if we read a book together before I leave and do something special when I get home?" Or, "Would you like to watch a movie with me or play a game before you go up to bed?" Establishing these rituals surrounding temporary breaks in parental presence will affirm the critical attachment connection that is growing between you and your child.

6. Never threaten your child verbally or physically, or with disruption of the adoption or displacement in foster care as a result of what you might assess as negative behavior.

Your foster or adopted child has come to you with this fear already intact. The stress and fear we carry with us as parents or caregivers in reaction to our child's difficult or confusing behaviors can push us past our coping limits. The result is the use of physical and emotional threats against our children.

In my 13 years of personal and professional experience in working with parents who foster and adopt children, I can verify that aggression in families will lead to more aggression, anger and fear in children. I am not alone in my research and observations. Several parenting experts agree.

Renowned pediatrician, Dr. T. Berry Brazelton, author of *Touchpoints, Your Child's Emotional and Behavioral Development*, Dr. William Sears, developer of Attachment Parenting and author of *The Discipline Book, How to have a Better Behaved Child*, Dr. Caron Goode, founder of the Academy for Coaching Parents International and designer of the Heart-Wise™ Parenting Model, and John Gottman, author of

Raising An Emotionally Intelligent Child, all agree that spanking and aggressive corporal punishments leveled against young children and teenagers are more likely to produce children and youth who are quicker to use hitting and other forms of violence to solve problems, including with their parents. Contemporary research provides strong consensus that most parents are quick to adopt kinder and more sensitive parenting styles when they are effectively introduced to alternative methods for positive discipline. Threats and punishments only reinforce prior harsh conditions in your child's memory and will further delay healthy bonding and attachment.

7. Speak to your child with a calm tone of voice and with words of affection.

Use terms of endearment when speaking with your child. This recommendation may seem superfluous, nevertheless, I urge you to accept it as a gentle reminder that all children consistently need to see, hear, and feel genuine affection from their caregivers. Use words or phrases like dear, honey, darling, or sweetheart. Use nicknames or pet names like pickles, sugarplum, or buddy. In the case of cross- cultural adoption, my favorites are: my spoonful of chocolate syrup, chocolate kiss, cinnamon, or my sweet little caramel drop!

Injecting lighthearted humor into the interaction will also ignite love and a sense of security in your child, especially in those tense teaching moments. For instance, my husband's grandfather, with whom he was very close, used the term 'little gangster' when referring to his grandson: "Come over here and sit next to me, you little gangster!" He would often say. It never failed to bring a wide smile to the heart and face of my husband when he was young, even when he was in trouble!

8. Maintain a relaxed and composed body posture and caring facial expressions in front of your child.

For the adult to sit down or otherwise lower themselves to the child's physical level during interactions helps empathy and bonding. This recommendation is especially valid during tense or stressful encounters between you and your child. Our natural or conditioned reaction is to stand over the child and proceed to lecture about their behavior, usually with our finger pointing directly in the face of the child. Presenting a relaxed and composed body posture and caring facial expressions will create security and invite trust and further communication.

To drive this principle home, take a few moments to stand in front of a mirror. Imagine that you are angry over something someone has done. It could be a co-worker, family member, or a child. Recall the incident and your emotions as vividly as you can. Close your eyes and feel the anger rise again inside, and begin to speak to the mirror the way you would speak to the other person or child. Now open your eyes and look at your facial expression. Scary? You get my point.

9. Always reassure your child you will seek solutions together.

You are able to help them through all their troubles, and your love and dedication to them is strong and genuine. How many ways can you do this?

10. Utilize adaptable rules and creative structure in the home and outside environment to effectively guide your child's behavior without becoming overly reactive, rigid, and punitive.

Example: The child becomes stubborn and defiant. When children are impacted by traumatic stress, this behavior is more defined. It signals to the parent that the child is moving into an area of inflexibility, and they will need the parent's patient assistance to work through it. This involuntary reaction is related to the freeze response in the brain and may manifest in various ways. Its core is a sense of personal threat and a horrific fear of loss. A young child may become rigid and resistant. An eight-year-old refuses to change activities or engage in tasks, and a teenager repeatedly fails to bathe due to stress before school. You are experiencing an inflexible child.

Reconsider your parental expectations during these times. If you understand that all children *want* to do well, and that they do well whenever they are able to, your decision to relax a rule or expectation will allow the child to grow in their ability to eventually accomplish it to meet your expectations. Children and youth benefit from patience, time and support to get unstuck. Allow the child additional time to process your request, with occasional prompts or reminders as your child can handle them. This is not the time to nag and lecture. The caution here is not to fall into sarcasm or feigned concern when dealing with this kind of behavior.

No matter what the age, you can join your child in the activity or task to be completed. Doing it together rather than expecting them to do it alone creates an easy transitional atmosphere. If the mood is right, throw in some music and dance your child into doing their chores! Teens will think you've lost your marbles, but it will lighten the stress and infuse some much-needed joy into the experience.

A Matter of Choice

It is highly recommended to allow for and offer two or more choices to the child. Let us take a moment to consider the above case of the teen resistant to bathing. How would you move him forward and out of his inflexible state?

- State your wish or expectation from the perspective of your genuine concern for him and his health, rather than from a platform of judgment, shame, or blame.

- Set your personal, parental frustration or anger aside. You can deal with that later. For example: "It is important to those around you that you bathe and feel good about yourself. I am concerned for your health if you do not bathe regularly, John. I would like it if you showered more frequently."

- Inquire if there is anything the young person or child needs to make it easier for them to accomplish the task. The goal is to help the child to feel unstuck, calm their anxiety, whether or not it is connected with the task, and enable them to make the transition more easily from one activity to the next. For example, "Is there anything special, perhaps a certain soap you are used to (or bubble bath for a younger child) you want me to buy for you?" "Do you need to make certain the door is locked?" "Do you need me to stay with you, or outside the door?" "What can I do to help you, dear?"

Remember that the underlying cause in this example is the stress the child experiences when going to school. It is this stress that has fixed him in a state of inflexibility, which extends to his ability to function well in other areas of life. He experiences it physically and emotionally as an unending cycle of fear or distress, which affects his ability to make decisions or think clearly. He likely will not know why he acts this way. His memories of the past may be confused. You will need to address this issue on three fronts:

- School attendance – Meet with teachers or others involved to seek solutions toward easing transition stress to and from school, and while at school.
- Issues with separation anxiety - use creative ways to reinforce safety.
- Self-care or bathing, which is how the stress of separation anxiety is manifesting itself in this instance.

Finally, offer clear choices without judgment or blame. "I can see you are having some difficulty with this request. Would you like to take your shower this evening or before school tomorrow?" If you are practicing flexibility in your parenting style, and are using adaptable rules and creative structure to guide your child, you will be more amenable to allowing a third choice. You will recognize that a third choice is warranted when you see that the child simply cannot come out of their state of inflexibility. "I know you are trying as best you can, dear. If you can't do it tonight or tomorrow morning, we can try this again at another time. For now I don't want you to worry about it."

What happens if the child cannot comply with your request and expectation over a period of time? How will you respond to this stressful situation? Which way will you travel? This is an important question because of the anxiety and frustration you will feel attempting to meet these unusual needs, and you will need to ask yourself this question repeatedly.

You can choose to react to this behavior by punishing, yelling, and removing privileges. Or you can choose to respond with a deeper understanding. As an adept parent-detective you pull the clues together to find a creative answer that will provide the most help for your child. You recall that heightened stress and fear in the body and mind can freeze a child into inactivity, or cause him or her to lash out at the ones they most dearly love even when they do not mean to. You remind yourself that with calculated planning and patient support from you, he or she will eventually gain back the resilience they once had to life. They will eventually overcome. Additionally, should you begin to recognize patterns in behavior, which may be detrimental or crippling to the child's healthy development, it is most important you bring these up to your health provider.

Discipline means to teach and guide. Above all, have patience, consistency, and flexibility! Create the right healing environment and love, trust, and connection will happen between you and your child.

> "A small child was asked, 'What is Love?'
> After some thought he answered,
> "I think you are supposed to be shot with an arrow or something,
> but the rest of it isn't supposed to be that painful."

Conclusion

When a child has a skewed perception of parental love and familial trust because of early experiences, the sensitive parent creates positive change in a child's thought, renews his or her reality, and uncovers the truth in their heart. You need only find the courage within you to do so, and the determination to stay the course! Lessons learned in transition, trust and love, whether before or after adoption, prepare and direct you toward your destination. What will happen when parents and child finally connect? One wonderful word...family! In chapter eight you will learn more about developmental trauma, what you need to look for, and how you can help.

Back Up & Restore

6 Actions of Remarkable Parents

What You Do For Your Children

1. Listen - More than just hearing, remarkable parents listen to their children. They hear beyond the words to the feelings their children mean to express. Remarkable parents listen.

2. Reflect - The ability to *wait* on intuition, experience, and wisdom, to discover the best ways to meet any challenge with their child. Remarkable parents reflect.

3. Are Mindful - Enter into an interaction with calm self-possession, aware of the power a parent has to influence rather than manipulate a child's behavior. Remarkable parents are mindful.

4. Attach - Act first to reconnect emotionally and physically with the child through loving interaction and healing, calming touch. Remarkable parents attach.

5. Respond - More than reacting, a thoughtful wise response will guide and inspire good behavior and heal strained connections between parent and child. Remarkable parents respond.

6. Bring Joy - Bring to daily life, activities which promote joy and happiness and cement good feelings into family relations. Remarkable parents bring joy.

Uncommon and Limitless Love Journal Activity

You now understand much more about the causes and triggers driving the behaviors of children from foster care. You now know the importance of understanding how transition, trust, and love affect your child, and you have healthy and positive parenting strategies to put in place to help your child better understand and cope with their behavioral responses.

Over the next week I want you to observe the emotions and behaviors of the children around you. Write in your journal how you interact with the children currently in your life.

- Can you recognize what emotions the child is feeling when they are upset, or are in need of adult guidance or supervision?

- Does your new awareness of a child's emotional state now influence how you think of your child or other children and how you choose to support to them?

- Use what you have learned in the previous chapter to write how you will give emotional support to the child with you now or soon to be placed.

- Practice meeting the child's internal and external needs without becoming angry or punishing toward the child. Let your creative parenting juices flow and keep humor in the mix.

ALTERNATE ROUTE

Trauma, Stress, & Attachment

"Trauma is perhaps the most avoided, ignored, belittled, denied, misunderstood, and untreated cause of human suffering."
~Dr. Bruce Perry, neuroscientist and international authority on children and trauma

While most children are instilled with an abundance of psychological and emotional resilience, some encounter great difficulties making the transition into adoption after pre-adoptive trauma. As mentioned in the previous chapter, these difficulties are unusual and intense behavioral displays, which could prove disruptive to family life. No book about adoption would be complete without a detour into these important issues of trauma, the impact of psychological and emotional stress, and your ability to heal your child.

In the last three decades, more attention has focused on children and trauma. Emerging neurological research on brain function has shed new light on how psychological and emotional stress and trauma affects the regulatory system of children, changes the brains' ability to function properly, and interrupts healthy development.[51] As parents, you want to expand your thinking of these critical points and how they may impact you and your child, so you will be better prepared to act wisely in the event you find yourselves on this alternate route.

What Is Trauma?

We most often associate the term trauma with a physical injury or what goes on in a hospital emergency room. This is only the surface effect, much like seeing the tip of an iceberg. The reality of what happens to the mind and body because of trauma is submerged beneath the surface, like the iceberg. Trauma, then, is not out of our minds because we cannot see surface symptoms.

In our nations recent emotional memory are devastating traumas like the aftermath of Hurricane Katrina and the Louisiana levee failures in 2005, the horrendous loss of life from the earthquakes and tsunami in Japan in 2011, and the unprecedented weather patterns that produced more than 600 tornadoes in the month of April 2011, obliterating entire towns from Virginia to Alabama, leaving over three hundred and forty persons dead and thousands injured and homeless. These certainly qualify as traumatic events. Our children's trauma is more than a catastrophic event.

Like tornadoes, trauma happens any time that the conditions are right, and genetics and temperament play a part like explaining why one person seems resilient and another person is devastated after a traumatic event. The effects of trauma damage some and leave others untouched. It can occur though the person experiencing the trauma is not physically present at the time of the traumatic event, as in watching video of the event on television, or hearing the repeated telling of a traumatic event by another person. Sadly recent history proves this to be true.

On a crystal blue morning in 2001, millions of Americans watched in horror as the unforgettable events of 9/11 unfolded on live television. As it became evident that our nation was under attack and innocent Americans were dying, the nation went into self-protect. Police and military were on high alert in every state, and as the word spread that a third plane hit the Pentagon, the FAA ordered all air traffic be grounded, and fighter jets flew cover for the first time in our history over New York and Washington, D.C.

In the aftershock, businesses closed and parents rushed to schools and day care centers to bring their children home. Communications failed as phone lines overloaded, and a stunned America and the international community sat glued to their television sets watching and hoping for survivors. Months after the attacks many Americans suffered from Post-Traumatic Stress, even though they lived and worked in states across the country and were nowhere near the East Coast, or our nation's Capital. Many people could not look up to see a plane in the sky, because it brought flashbacks of the passenger jets flying into the towers of the World Trade Center. They were not near to the events, nor did they have anyone they knew personally. Yet, the viewing of constant television images and the accompanying emotional fear that settled deep in mind and body traumatized them.

Neuroscience tells us that our ability or inability to express, understand, and process life-shattering events indicates whether or not trauma leaves its dark mark on the body mind system. Biophysicist Dr. Peter Levine states in his book *Waking the Tiger, Healing Trauma:* "Trauma is not in the event itself, rather, trauma resides in the nervous system." Any shocking or scary event has the potential to produce trauma and stress in the body, whenever our neurophysiology is triggered to believe it is in a life-threatening environment.[52] In other words, any sudden, overwhelming, or repeating emotional or physical event has the ability to leave devastating emotional and psychological effects.

Recent Studies

In 2001, the horrendous tragedy of 9/11 brought renewed attention to how children experience traumatic stress and its effects on their lives. According to studies by the New York School of Medicine, "1.2 million children from New York City were directly affected by the 9/11 attacks."[53] Prominent scientists, neurologists, and psychologists throughout the United States began intensive studies on the effects of trauma on these children.

Studies focused on school-aged kids from 6-18 years. The surprising results revealed that children with no prior psychopathology developed significant life-crippling fears with diagnosable psychological and behavioral disorders after the 9/11 events. Some of these disorders developed within one month of the attacks. Those noted in a New York Board of Education Study released 6 months after the attacks were, Post Traumatic Stress Disorder, major depression, panic, separation anxiety, and conduct disorder.

One year after this study, one in every six children continued to experience nightmares, bedwetting, fears of losing parents, fears of going out, and aversion to school buses. There was a notable increase in risk-taking behaviors among the group's teenagers disproportionate to the general adolescent population. Rises in cigarette smoking, drug and alcohol involvement, and oppositional behavior were prevalent, along with marked decline in academics. While 40% of the approximately 8000 school children in New York City were affected because they personally witnessed or were injured in the attacks, about 30% of the children diagnosed with the above disorders watched the coverage on TV.[54]

The sudden, catastrophic effects that traumatic stress leaves on the mind and body of children is understood clearly as a result of this and other intensive studies following the 9/11 attacks. There is continuing recent independent research that shows direct relationship between early traumatic stress and its lasting effects on the neurological and physical health of both child and adult.[55]

This wealth of information provides great hope for the future mental health of children coming from traumatic life history, but only if we know how to apply it effectively. With this knowledge at our fingertips, what are the questions we must now ask?

· What are the warnings signs in our children?
· Can we prevent it?
· Can we heal the pain?

Signs or Symptoms of Trauma

On June 10, 2002, Charles Curie, the Administrator of SAMHSA, The Substance Abuse and Mental Health Services Administration, which is part of the U.S. Department of Health and Human Services, addressed the Senate Committee on Health, Education, Labor and Pensions. His speech focused on "The Effects of Trauma on Children and the Role of Mental Health Services." The following excerpt from his statement to the committee is a list of "Trauma Reactions Possible in Children and Adolescents."

Although the list is divided into age groups, reactions can span developmental stages. For instance, increased self-focusing and withdrawal, or rebellion at home and school mentioned in the Adolescent category may also be seen in

Young Children 1-6. Similarly, some families with youth 12-18 years experience regressive symptoms like bedwetting in the 1-6 year old category and separation anxiety from the 6-11 year old category. This list is offered in order to awaken your awareness of the many ways overwhelming fear, stress and trauma can manifest in the behaviors of children. When you can recognize the signs you can get help.

Possible Trauma Reactions in Children and Adolescents

"Young Children (1-6)
· Helplessness and passivity, lack of usual responsiveness
· Generalized fear
· Heightened arousal and confusion
· Difficulty talking about event, lack of verbalization
· Difficulty identifying feelings
· Nightmares and other sleep disturbances
· Regressive symptoms (e.g. bedwetting, loss of acquired speech and motor skills)
· Inability to understand death as permanent
· Grief related to abandonment by caregiver
· Somatic symptoms (e.g. stomach aches, headaches)
· Startle response to loud or unusual noises
· Fussiness, uncharacteristic crying, and neediness
· Avoidance of or alarm response to specific trauma-related reminders involving sights and physical sensations

School-aged Children (6-11)
· Feelings of responsibility and guilt
· Repetitious traumatic play and retelling
· Feeling disturbed by reminders of the event

- Nightmares and other sleep disturbances
- Concerns about safety and preoccupation with danger
- Aggressive behavior and angry outbursts
- Fear of feelings and trauma reactions
- Close attention to parents' anxieties
- Withdrawal, school avoidance
- Worry and concern for others
- Somatic symptoms (complaints about bodily aches and pains)
- Obvious anxiety and fearfulness
- Specific trauma-related fears; general fearfulness
- Regression (behaving like a younger child)
- Separation anxiety
- Loss of interest in activities
- Confusion and inadequate understanding of traumatic events (more evident in play than in discussion)
- Unclear understanding of death and the causes of "bad" events
- Giving magical explanations to fill in gaps in understanding
- Loss of ability to concentrate at school, with lowering of performance
- "Spacey" or distractible behaviors

Pre-adolescents and Adolescents (12-18)
- Self-consciousness
- Life-threatening reenactment
- Rebellion at home or school
- Abrupt shift in relationships
- Depression and social withdrawal
- Decline in school performance

- Trauma-driven acting out, such as with sexual activity and reckless risk taking
- Effort to distance oneself from feelings of shame, guilt, and humiliation
- Excessive activity and involvement with others, or retreat from others in order to manage inner turmoil
- Accident proneness
- Wish for revenge and action-oriented responses to trauma
- Increased self-focusing and withdrawal
- Sleep and eating disturbances, including nightmares"[56]

Caution Signs

It is very important to remember that not all children are affected equally by the experience of traumatic life events, but all are affected to some extent. To understand and recognize possible signs of trauma in foster or adopted children, a parent or caregiver must have three things:

1. A moderate knowledge of your child's history prior to placement

2. Awareness of any continued high stress situations after placement, such as, changing schools, ongoing parental visitation or court procedures, and even your parenting style

3. Attention to the wide range of subtle to severe behavioral cues as listed above

As a parent, you need to know that the processes occurring within the mind and body governing your child's reactions to you, or to the environment whether home, school, or neighborhood, is:

- Stress related
- Internally triggered by the external environment, and
- Not within your child's ability to control

Certain brain-based stress responses, known as flight, fight, and freeze occur automatically, become highly sensitive as a result of trauma, and are part of the built-in survival mechanisms we all share. Centered within our brains' Limbic System, these mechanisms are fear-triggered and are fired deep within the brain. They exist solely for our self-preservation and to secure our sense of personal safety in the world. The reality is that the child placed with you may be vulnerable to typical or high stress interactions due to early life experiences.[57] In some cases a child's traumatic experience has left them vulnerable to life. Vulnerability may continue long after placement is made, because the child's physiology is already in a state of overwhelm and their sensitivity to daily stress is excessively heightened.

Above all, it is important for you, as the caregiver, to know that your child is seeking to regain their internal sense of security while it may not immediately appear to you that this is the case. All parents benefit from a basic understanding of how the brain and the autonomic nervous system works to protect the body, and how stress and fear can dominate a child's reactions and behaviors, and override their cognitive ability. You can use this powerful knowledge to parent your foster or adopted child with love, compassion, and success, even in the toughest situations.

Awareness, education, and preparation bring greater confidence and strength to you. The knowledge that your child may come with a traumatic history is not cause for panic. Research shows how the *distressed physiology* of the child is directly and positively affected by the *calm physiology* of the caregiver. Continue to enhance those skills to provide loving support and parent your child from a calm body and mind.[58]

Summary

From previous chapters you have learned much. You have already traveled far. You have looked honestly at your emotional pain and disappointment from past broken relationships or infertility. You surrounded your family with strong support systems, and through the practice of right mindfulness and deep breathing, you have gained personal awareness on how to meet your needs so you can meet the needs of your child. You can feel secure in the knowledge that your personal growth work balances your emotions and wellbeing, and serves you well in parenting your adopted child.

If you think you see signs that your child is displaying odd, unusual, detached, withdrawn, or unexpected behaviors, or if your child seems frequently overwhelmed in certain situations, you may wish to speak with your pediatrician or family doctor. Do not hesitate to call on my coaching services and together we can explore the right resolutions for your family. Help is never far away.

Caregivers as Healing Agents

"Whenever we go through a traumatic event a vital part of our spiritual essence, our soul (spirit), separates from us in order to survive and avoid feeling the full impact of physical and emotional pain. After the loss has occurred, the trauma is over... and we feel safe again, we forget to "pick up" the pieces we left behind. We move on with our life not realizing that a part of us is missing. We compensate or cover for the part that is gone. We know something is wrong but we don't know what."

~Phil Morgan, "Reclaiming Our Wholeness"

It is our duty as loving parents and nurturing caregivers to help restore our child's sense of safety and wholeness in the world, and to begin to heal the ruptures in their false perception of what relationship means. Children, who have suffered loss by any measure, become estranged from the feeling that their life is secure. In the blank face of this fact, how can their sense of security be restored? Notwithstanding the complex elements of family-based or community mental health supports, which combine in this regard, I firmly believe through my experience, that stable and well-regulated caregivers can and must become the primary healing agents in a child's life. Using the components of secure attachment and emotional bonding, trained resource and adoptive parents can focus on meeting their child's deepest needs for safety and security, and promote critical emotional healing.

Emotional Bonding & Secure Attachment

Early research on attachment developed initially as a theory through the work of eminent British psychologist, John Bowlby, who was later joined by Mary Ainsworth in 1950. It was Ainsworth, who first developed the security theory, which states that the child in the early stages of developmental growth is emotionally and psychologically dependent upon its secure connection with its caregivers. The attachment figure is primarily the mother, although there is expanded evidence that fathers, grandparents, and siblings equally fit into this model as strong attachment figures. The quality of empathy in the child-parent interactions and connection promotes healthy brain development in the child.

Healthy brain development translates into a well attached, secure, and internally regulated child. This child can easily access its internal resources to self-soothe, has developed internal resilience, and can branch out with confidence into the world or onto the playground. His or her belief in their personal security is present because they know that each time they turn to look back, a caring, vigilant, and present parent will be there. Ainsworth stated that where this familial secure attachment is lacking "the individual is handicapped by a lack of what might be called a *secure base.*"[59]

In the previous chapter under TRUST, I listed the essential physical and emotional needs of all children. Within this list are the components of healthy bonding and secure attachment. They are really quite simple.

- Responsive care and predictability

- Physical and tender affection from caregivers

- Secure and uncompromised connection with other human beings

- A structured environment where safety, learning, and spiritual growth can happen

- And lastly, the golden keys of joy through play and laughter

You may consider the above elements, the 'Rolls Royce' of healthy emotional bonding and secure attachment in all families. We recognize that some children come into foster care and adoption marked with deep wounds from familial trauma and loss. We also recognize and advocate that with services aimed at preemptive prevention and targeted education provided to adoptive and resource parents, not all wounds have to become life-disfiguring scars.

"If a community values its children,
it must cherish their parents."
~John Bowlby

Conclusion

A child's connection with a loving, supportive, and attachment-aware caregiver creates opportunities each day for healing past trauma through the gift of uncommon love. Relationship and our loving and constant presence is the healing key. Sometimes our work as caregivers is not for the faint of heart. But, you will never know what you are made of until you step into the fire. Step bravely!

> *"Fire can warm or consume,*
> *water can quench or drown,*
> *wind can caress or cut.*
> *And so it is with human relationships;*
> *we can both create and destroy,*
> *nurture and terrorize,*
> *traumatize and heal each other"*
> ~ Bruce D. Perry

Back Up & Restore

NOT IN MY HOUSE!

Closing the Door on Reactive Parenting

No parent begins their journey deciding to be harsh or hurtful as part of their parenting plan. The irony of parenthood is that we sometimes *react* to our children in negative ways that defy our natural parenting instincts. Comedienne Phyllis Diller expresses this thought with humor when she says: "We spend the first twelve months of our children's lives teaching them to walk and talk, and the next twelve telling them to sit down and shut up."

Do you react more than you respond to your child? If so, it is time you close the door on reactive parenting. This is the right time for parent's to say, "Not in my house!"

Generational Conditioning

"Don't push my buttons!"

There are one or more painful childhood experiences hiding beneath our so-called buttons. We heard harsh words from our parents or teachers, and they heard them from their parents...back through the generations. These painful remembrances are just below our seemingly calm parental exterior.

Any every-day event is capable of exposing the painful scars on the heart of the child still within us. As our daily demands and stress levels stretch, there remains the likely potential of a rupture of our unresolved hurts. When our buttons pop, they reveal a lot about why we react, and we say words that come straight from generational conditioning.

The following is a list of conditioned phrases. Don't be surprised if some of them sound familiar to you.
- Not in my house!
- Over my dead body!
- Not if I have anything to say about it?
- Don't give me that attitude!
- Wipe that smirk off your face before I wipe it for you!
- Don't give me that look!
- Don't talk to me with that tone!
- Stop crying or I'll give you something to cry about.
- I tell you till I'm blue in the face.
- Listen to me or else...
- Do as I say or else...
- Sit there until you figure out what you did.
- Go to your room! I don't want to see you.
- Say that again and I'll wash your mouth out with soap!
- Are you stupid? What were you thinking?
- If Jimmy jumped off a bridge would you do it too?
- It doesn't matter what you think (or feel) I make the rules.
- In this house you'll do as I say.

And, of course, the all-time parental favorite:
- Because I said so!

Whew! Even I have to breathe through reading that list!

The Parenting Paradox

*"We all grow up with the weight of history on us.
Our ancestors dwell in the attics of our brains
as they do in the spiraling chains of knowledge hidden
in every cell of our bodies."*
~Shirley Abbott

The heart of the parenting journey is the joy of creating family and pro-active parenting, protecting, teaching, and nurturing. As new foster and adoptive parents you now have an opportunity to make decisions about how to parent your children. As you look at the personal knowledge and experience you have gathered about parenting throughout your life, you now carefully weigh which beliefs and practices to keep from past generations, those practices you will amend in the light of new information, and the healthiest parenting approaches to adopt from advanced and contemporary research. Your new and improved parenting philosophy grows from what you now value most.

Each of the above phrases communicates a very powerful negative message to our children. The message is one of parental power and control over our children through fear, threats, and isolation. These damaging messages are certainly not what we had in mind when we decided to become parents. These are not the messages we ever intended to give, and if they once were, you now have the chance to change them.

Challenge & Growth

It is important to know that we do not give these negative messages to our children willingly, or even consciously. Each one of us carries within us emotional echoes from past generations. The way we interact with and speak to our children is heavily seeded by early childhood experiences with our own caregivers. This generational conditioning does not mean we cannot improve on experiences of our past by deciding to change the way in which we treat our children now and in the future.

Life is about challenge and growth. Challenge is our willingness to explore and acknowledge our actions without further injury of self-blame. Challenge is simply to know, accept, and move forward. Growth is our readiness and ability to move beyond the obstacle. Growth is active. It requires participation.

Are you ready to close the door on conditioned reactive parenting? Okay. This is your part. You say, "Yes! I am!"

Out With the Old

Great! It is time to take charge of the parent you want to be. Here are six positive things to tell your child, which will help you replace your old conditioning with new.

1. You are such a great kid. I am so glad I have you.

2. We are very proud of you for _____. Fill in your child's accomplishment. Such as: I am very proud of you for taking good care of the dog; or, for trying hard on your test.

3. Life is an experiment. You will make mistakes, but you will never disappoint me.

4. Don't ever be afraid to come to me for help or support.

5. I'll always be here to listen.

6. I love you.

Reactive Parenting? Not in my house!

DEBORAH A. BEASLEY

HONORING CULTURE IN
TRANSRACIAL ADOPTIONS

Let the Soul Searching Begin!

"One day our descendants will think it incredible that we paid so much attention to things like the amount of melanin in our skin or the shape of our eyes or our gender instead of the unique identities of each of us as complex human beings."

~Franklin Thomas, former President and CEO of
The Ford Foundation and head of the TFF Study Group,
assisting development in South Africa

If we are opening our hearts to children who are culturally or ethnically different from ourselves, there is soul searching to be done to prepare our hearts and homes for this transition. According to the latest research statistics from The Evan B. Donaldson Adoption Institute, nearly 15% of the 36,000 domestic U.S. adoptions in 1998 were transracial or transcultural. The numbers of interracial adoptions are on the rise; up from 8% in 1987.[60] Three important questions need to be asked and answered in the minds of transracially adopting parents.

- How do I plan to honor the ethnicity and cultural heritage of my children?
- What part does cultural identity play in the development of healthy self-esteem?
- What part do parents' racial or cultural attitudes play in the enculturation of their adopted children?

This chapter will address these and other issues surrounding interracial adoption.

Take a moment to consider how you describe yourself to others who have never seen you? What attributes or values do you claim when telling others about yourself? Do you wake up or go through your day with a vivid consciousness of what color or race you are, or where you will feel comfortable in the family, neighborhood, society, or country in which you live? Are there places you cannot go for fear of a lack of acceptance? Are you frequently searching to find others who share the same features as you? Do you wonder what others think when they see you?

These are some of the questions and uncertainties, which are part of the daily experiences of many transcultural or transracial adopted kids. Making the decision to adopt transracially will personally place you face to face with the difficult social issues of racial and ethnic discrimination, tolerance and acceptance. Let the soul searching begin!

If you have had little or no personal connection with these issues or you have been able to avoid them up to now in your life, you are in for quite an adventure! As acclaimed screen actress, Betty Davis, once said, "Buckle up, folks...it's going to be a bumpy ride!"

TRANSRACIAL ADOPTION

*"When I was little I never thought about being around so many
white people, it was just my life and I'm happy where I am.
As I get older it matters more because I don't see too many people
like me. Sometimes I forget I'm black. I forget I'm different ...
until one of my friends reminds me, or I catch my reflection in a
mirror. Mostly, I try not to let things like that get into my head.
I want to keep focused on my life and my future. If it gets into my
head it will mess me up, and I can't let that happen. I know that
staying me is being me."*

~12 year old African American Adoptee, Florida

With few exceptions the majority of transracial adoptions in the United States will include white parents of European decent and racial or ethnic minority children.[61] In 2001, the U.S. Department of Health and Human Services reported that 75,722 children (60%) out of the 127,000 children waiting to be adopted from foster care were of Hispanic, African American, Asian American, and Native American decent. International adoptions account for approximately 85% of all transracial adoptions in the United States.[62]

Transracial adoption (also referred to as transcultural and interracial) is undeniably the most visible of all forms of adoption because the physical differences between the adoptive parents and adoptee are more apparent. As such, your newly formed multicultural family can expect to draw more attention whenever you are in public. More attention may also mean unwanted and unsolicited racial comments from strangers, whether in the mall or the supermarket. I am always amazed when strangers ask intrusive questions within the hearing distance of my two African American adopted children.

This is an occurrence that same race adoptive parents do not share. Same race adoptive parents are instances where both the adoptive parents and adopted children share the same race, for instance, Caucasian parents adopting a Caucasian child or Hispanic parents adopting a Hispanic child. Additionally comments may come in the form of compliments and admiration. My husband and I received these most often from persons or couples of our child's cultural background. Complete strangers would approach us, warmly introduce each member of their family by name, shake our hands, physically embrace us, and introduce themselves to our children. This humbling and unexpected experience always bolstered our confidence in what was otherwise a foreign land!

Relationship – Honoring the Tie That Binds

A break in any connection is a break in relationship. Children adopted across races and cultures, whether as domestic or international adoptees, often struggle to connect with where they belong. They live between two worlds, and can be painfully conscious of obvious external differences. They share fully in the culture of their adoptive family while desiring to know and experience their own. As if being adopted were not difficult enough, loss of culture, language, heritage, and ethnic pride deepens their sense of separation. We cannot allow our children to struggle alone in their efforts to connect with their heritage. For our children's sake we cannot be colorblind.[63]

The above quote from a young adoptee reflects the experience of being separated from their birth culture as well as their steady resolve and courage to push beyond the sharp reality of racial differences and prejudice and into the future. This resolve has not happened by chance. An empirical evidence shows that the quality of cultural and ethnic exposure adoptive parents provide to their transracially-adopted children is directly related to positive psychological adjustment and the formation of a positive, ethnic, and cultural identity. This is especially true when adoptive parents actively promote their children's ethnic cultures.[64] Parents who promote their child's culture help them to develop ethnic pride and confidence which translates into the necessary coping and survival skills needed to navigate racism in American society.

External Influences

How we experience culture, and what we believe about our culture, heritage, and ethnicity is relevant to the following considerations.

- Our parents' interactions and relationship with their heritage
- Values instilled in us as children from parents and community
- Traditions and customs practiced in the family
- Positive or negative social and cultural imprints
- Personal sense of inclusion through association and relationship with our specific ethnicities

Internal Influences

Even when we are raised with minimal external cultural influences, which reflect our family traditions and heritage, subtle nuances of generational traditions, societal mores, and social customs influence every fiber of our being. Use your Uncommon and Limitless Love Journal to answer the following questions to help let the soul searching begin.

- What have I been told or taught throughout my life about my child's cultural or ethnic social group, both positive and negative? Has this information come to me verbally or by innuendo from others?
- How do I really feel about people from my child's ethnic/cultural background? This is an opportunity for personal growth. Make it real and be honest in your exploration of these issues.

Those of us who are older and grew up in the decades before the civil rights movement remember being raised in a far less inclusive society. I grew up in an American society that could not tolerate persons of color to aspire to the same freedoms as whites. Racial prejudice was a cancerous infection in the social fabric even as the civil rights movement was advancing. This was an era where it was sadly fashionable to make jokes, degrading others with derogatory terms, no matter what their nationality or ethnic origin.

We remember the heroic courage of Rosa Parks, who refused to give up her seat in the front of a bus because of a social misbelief that *her* human dignity was somehow less than that of any other person. Our nightly news brought images of fire hoses and dogs turned on blacks in the streets of Atlanta because they desired to be accepted as equal, but were not treated as such. Mistrust and fear of those unlike us, no matter what color, ran a sad but strong undercurrent beneath the hearts of many.

Now is the time to examine ourselves, as we prepare to welcome our children home at last. Even as we profess to rise above old social ideas and prejudices, the silent influences of past times are still somewhere within us. To prevent that ugly sleeping dog from emerging suddenly in the midst of an angry outburst, we must wake and drag him into the light to deal fully and honestly with him *before* we bring our children home. We must put that old dog completely out of its misery and move on.

· What are our relatives' or friends' reactions to our adopting children of a culture or race different from our own?

If we are conditioned by past and present social climates, so are those around us. It is time to have those heart-to-heart talks with extended family members and close friends. We *want* to know what our family thinks of our decision to adopt cross-culturally. We do not live in a vacuum, but in family units and communities. No matter how far we are spread across the country, we turn to family for support, approval, acceptance and love. As adoptive parents we love and accept our children. We fully accept who they are in all their beautiful differences. But, what will we do if a close family member cannot accept our decision and our new children?

I was afraid of this same issue when we brought our first African American daughter home. I witnessed a most touching event at a family gathering. An elderly uncle grabbed my daughter up on his knee and began smothering her with kisses.

"Look at you," he said, grinning and rubbing her arms.

"Look at your skin! How beautiful it is!" At that moment my tears washed all my fears about how my children would be accepted by my family. I forgot to remember this simple truth:

"People change and forget to tell each other."
~Lillian Hillman, American Playwright

Are You Culturally Competent?

Cultural competence is not mastered in a single introduction or course. It is an understanding and respect for other races and cultures not our own acquired over the course of a lifetime. In her groundbreaking research on *Cultural Competence for Transracial Adoptive Parents*, Dr. Elizabeth Vonk from the University of Ohio sites three primary constructs toward the development of cultural competency in adoptive parents: Multicultural Planning, Survival Skills and Racial Awareness"[65]

Multicultural Planning refers to ways in which an adoptee might come in contact with his or her birth culture and what opportunities they might have to participate with others of their same race or ethnicity on a regular basis.[66] Begin thinking now about this plan and investigate community options for cultural interaction. Although it may constitute a significant change in thought (and comfort level), there are many ideas to consider. Return to your journal to answer these questions.

- Is there a community near you that reflects your child's culture?

- Is there a community center, Heritage center, or college, that hosts multicultural celebrations and events?

- Are there local churches, temples, or houses of worship with strong ties to your child's ethnic background to allow your family future opportunities to visit or participate as guests or as part of the church family?

Not long ago I had the privilege of speaking with fourteen-year-old Deshawn on the topic of his experience growing up. A Caucasian couple adopted Deshawn when he was 3 years old. They live in a primarily white neighborhood and Deshawn attends a primarily white school. I asked this bright, cheery young man if he would share from his perspective what challenges or concerns African-American kids in his circumstances faced. With little hesitation he answered his greatest fear was that he would not be able to find a college or a job that would accept him. This surprised me and I asked him to explain further.

He responded, "Everywhere I go I fail to see many people like myself. There is no one like me that works in the dentist's office, our doctor's office, or at school. I just wonder how other people like me can get a good job and earn a living." This young man deduced that since he could not see many African Americans in professional positions in his immediate neighborhood perhaps they could not access higher education and therefore were not able to acquire professional positions of employment. The unspoken message received by Deshawn in his neighborhood altered his belief in his ability to achieve a promising future.

I suggested that due to his narrow experiences with persons of his ethnicity he necessarily had only a narrow view of the truth. I asked Deshawn to consider the bigger picture by helping him to identify prominent persons of color in his broader environment. He was able to relate to prominent business and local television personalities who lived in the vicinity of his town. From this exercise Deshawn gained a new perspective and assurance in his ability to attain whatever he reached for in his future, educationally and professionally.

Below is the first of three parent checklists excerpted with permission from Dr. Elizabeth Vonk's significant research in transracial adoption. She suggests that "TRA, or

Transracially Adoptive Parents build a bridge between their own and their child's race and culture."[67] She offers the following 14 recommendations to assist for a multicultural plan. If you are adopting transracially, how many can you check off?

1. "I include regular contact with people of other races and cultures in my life.

2. I place my children in multicultural schools.

3. I place my children with teachers who are racially aware and skilled with children of my child's race.

4. I understand how my choices about where to live affect my child.

5. I have developed friendships with families and individuals of color who are good role models for my children.

6. I purchase books, toys, and dolls that are like my child.

7. I include traditions from my child's birth culture in my family celebrations.

8. I provide my children with opportunities to establish relationships with adults from their birth culture.

9. I provide my children with the opportunity to learn the language of their birth culture.

10. I provide my children with the opportunity to appreciate the music of their birth culture.

11. I have visited the country or community of my child's birth.

12. I have demonstrated the ability for sustained contact with members of my child's racial or ethnic group.

13. I seek services and personal contacts in the community that will support my child's ethnicity.

14. I live in a community that provides my child with same-race adult and peer role models on an ongoing basis."

"I was having trouble with some kids at my school. Whenever they saw me they would make racial jokes. The hurtful thing was that everyone else thought it was funny too. It hurt me a lot and I asked them repeatedly to stop. I noticed that a few teachers would make excuses for it like it was a mistake, or not done on purpose. I finally told someone I could trust and they helped me."

~Middle school student and interracial adoptee, Pennsylvania

Survival Skills refers to the responsibility of adoptive parents to equip transracially-adopted children with knowledge and abilities that will help them cope success-fully in the face of prejudice and discrimination.[68] As adoptive caregivers and members of a society, which is both rich in cultural diversity as it is with racial prejudice, we must acknowledge this reality and furnish our children with the strength of character needed to rise above racial injustice and meet their ultimate life goals.

Opening the conversation about race and discrimina-tion with your child may initially feel difficult and awkward. Nevertheless, this conversation needs to begin early and often in your child's life. My own child began to experience racial discrimination at the age of three years, when another child called her the "n" word. If you and your child do not share the same heritage you will need to make concerted efforts to learn their cultural history of oppres-sion and discrimination accurately in order to relate to what they are experiencing. The truth is your child will inevitably experience discrimination and racism, and they will have to learn how to respond and not to internalize what is done or said against them as a reflection of their worth. Adoptive parents and others in the immediate family will also be on the receiving end of the same types of discrimination and racial ignorance as your child. You must learn to recognize when it is present, no matter how subtle, and understand how best to deal with it. Even though your child may be too young to understand the full impact of another's discriminatory actions toward them, you must take up the standard of defense on behalf of your child. The following stories illustrate three transracial foster-adoptive families' experiences with racial prejudice, bigotry, and discrimination, and share how they responded.

Tony and Clare's story is told by Toni: We were brand new foster parents when our child was first placed with us. We are white and she is black. We fell in love with her the moment we laid eyes on her. I guess we were naïve in the early days, and we were unprepared for the absurd remarks some people make. We never experienced racial prejudice before and it caught us by surprise.

We took our beautiful two-month old little girl for a walk through a shopping district in a nearby town. We felt proud to be with her and wanted to show her off in her new duds and bonnet. Several people passing by greeted us with the customary smiles and nods you receive as new parents, and then an older woman approached the carriage. She stuck her head right in the carriage above the peacefully sleeping baby. Her grin suddenly disappeared, and as she straightened up, this is what she had to say. "Oh! You must be babysitting." The woman shifted away from the carriage and closer to my wife and me as if we all had an intimate secret to share, and she stated the following, "Look at her hands and feet!" We automatically smiled presuming she would say how cute the baby's tiny hands were. Boy, were we wrong! She continued while edging closer and lowering her voice, "Did you ever look at the palms of *their* hands and soles of *their* feet? They're white! Did you ever notice that?"

The polite smiles on our faces froze and quickly faded as we realized the true colors of this woman standing so near to us. We instinctively backed away from the woman and my wife replied sharply, "Really! What is it you are trying to say about our child? I don't get it!" The woman stood straight up with a wide eyed look of indignation, shifted her gaze to me and back to my wife, then she stalked off with an audible huff. I suppose she came to the realization that we did not have anything in common after all.

Jessie and daughter Genna'a story: My newly adopted four-year-old African American daughter, Genna, had an appointment with a specialist, and we were sitting in the office waiting for her turn to see the doctor. The office was very crowded and there were moms and kids everywhere. When they called our name, I took Genna by the hand and started toward the front desk. Before I could reach the desk the woman sitting behind it shouted across the room. "Foster?" I looked up not really hearing what she said. She repeated it louder. "Foster?" She said, this time pointing vehemently toward my daughter. As I reached the desk area, she repeated it in a loud tone as if I were hard of hearing. "Foster child?" I breathed deeply and flatly corrected her.

As we walked toward the exam room my little daughter asked what the word foster meant. "They called us by the wrong name, mommy. They must mean somebody else," she said. For the sake of my daughter I did not make a fuss over the incident, as my daughters health became my priority in the moment. We spent about an hour and a half with the doctor and it gave me some time to reflect on how I was going to handle this situation. When our visit was over, I took a deep breath and approached the front desk. I requested to speak to the woman who had registered and called us up for the appointment, as well as the office manager. I demanded a formal apology by both of them for how they treated my daughter. "If my daughter was my color, you would never have considered making such a distinction. You insulted, confused, embarrassed, and singled my daughter out, and you did it in a public and very noticeable way. You presumed my daughter is a foster child because I am white and she is African American, even though we share the same last name. You presumed too much in error. How do you know my husband is not black? My daughter and I expect an apology for your mistake."

I spoke to them with more respect than they had afforded my daughter. I was angry and spoke with force, and without raising my voice. I wanted them to see a different perspective. I think I got my point across. Not only did they genuinely apologize to my daughter and me in the office, but also, I received a formal letter of apology two days later and information about where to make a complaint report if I chose to. I chose not to make the report. The letter and raising their consciousness toward others who would come to their office after us was enough for me.

A lesson from the author's personal experience: My family and I love to go camping in our travel trailer. We consider it a wonderful wholesome way to explore nature, see the sights in other states, and build great family memories. On one recent camping excursion we were blatantly reminded how selectively prejudice some people can be.

While making reservations for a long weekend stay at a popular out of state campground, I had a pleasant telephone conversation with the owner's wife. Our family visited this particular campground many times in years past when our older children were small, and I reminisced with her about our previously memorable camping experiences. I requested information about camping with them the following entire season. After settling the details in several friendly and personable phone conversations, we decided we would bring the deposit for our seasonal campsite at our

Successful Foster Care Adoption

upcoming weekend visit.

It was dark when we arrived and my husband registered two adults and two children at the office, while the kids and I remained in the car. While in the office my husband confirmed our reservation for the next season and was told he could pay the deposit before leaving. We had a great time while we were there, hiking backwoods trails, telling scary stories by the campfire, and of course, making s'mores. On the third day of our stay, we took a walk to the camp store. I noticed that the woman behind the counter and the owner's wife asked subtle and prying questions about our kids. I recognized the subtlety as being more than polite curiosity about adoption, and my answers became deliberately vague.

My husband walked throughout the small store picking out the items he needed. The girl's moseyed slowly through the store following after their dad. As kids often do, they picked up small toys curiously or fingered candy and other tempting items on shelves. I noticed that the eyes of both women behind the counter kept darting toward the kids as they walked through the aisles.

As I stood at the counter making small talk with the owner's wife, my older daughter, 11, asked if we would purchase a certain key chain for her souvenir. Like any good parent, I suggested she ask her dad. My daughter took the key chain off the display and skipped toward the back of the store where her dad stood. The owner's wife, who was facing me on the opposite side of the glass counter, watched my daughter intently all the while. In fact, she forgot she was talking and bent her body completely across the counter in order not to lose visual sight of my daughter and the key chain.

"Is there a problem?" I asked facetiously. She was so absorbed in her mission she did not answer me right away.

147

"Oh, no. I was just checking something."

"I can see that," I said.

"No problem," she repeated.

"Really? Because it seems there *is* a problem."

"No, not at all." The owner's wife replied.

We purchased ice cream for the kids. I took the key chain from my daughter and replaced it prominently in front of the woman and we left.

The final morning of our stay, when it was time to check out, I went to the office to pay our deposit for the next year's seasonal campsite. The owner's wife strongly suggested that we wait until next year so we would be certain we want to come back. I feigned confusion.

"We enjoyed ourselves so much, and I have the full deposit ready to give you. It's no problem. In fact, I would rather do it now," I explained.

She answered me quietly and deliberately, "I couldn't put you near anyone older." (*We're older,* I thought to myself.) "You have children, and it would be disturbing to older campers."

I countered just as deliberately. "My children are very quiet and well behaved. Here is my deposit."

She bounced right back at me, "The truth is, I am not certain this early what spaces would be available. I think it would be best if I sent you a letter listing the available sites for next season as they become available, and you can then decide if you want to come back. After all, we may not have a space you will be happy with."

I tried with dogged determination to book the site and pay her. I persisted long enough that the other woman working there tried to intervene, by agreeing with the owner's wife, and adding reasons why we should wait. I persisted long enough that they both became uncomfortable and were totally running out of made up excuses for why it would be better not to book a vacation there. I am wise to this stuff now, folks. As sad as it is for adoptive or foster families (and anyone of color or minority in the United States) to have to endure this treatment, we still have to make the point that we recognize what's going on and this kind of behavior is not acceptable. Needless to say, we will not be camping there again.

How you choose to address these issues will deeply affect your child. They will model themselves after your responses. In teaching our children to be strong and proud, we cannot allow our children or us to fall into a pit of anger and retaliation toward others. Nor can parents become indifferent, thereby minimizing the child's painful, fearful, and confusing exposure to discrimination. Parents cannot allow the experience of discrimination to rob them or their children of their power to rise above and beyond.

> *"Out of the huts of history's shame, I rise*
> *Up from a past that's rooted in pain, I rise...*
> *... Bringing the gifts that my ancestors gave*
> *I am the dream and the hope of the slave,*
> *I rise, I rise, I rise."*
> ~Maya Angelou

Here are 13 more points from Elizabeth Vonk to enhance your awareness of the importance of teaching racial survival skills in your family.

1. "I educate my children about the realities of racism and discrimination.

2. I help my children cope with racism through open and honest discussion in our home about race and oppression.

3. I am aware of the attitudes of friends and family members toward my child's racial and cultural differences.

4. I am aware of a variety of strategies that can be used to help my child cope with acts of prejudice or racism.

5. I know how to handle unique situations, such as my child's attempts to alter his or her physical appearance to look more like family members or friends.

6. I help my children recognize racism.

7. I help my children develop pride in themselves.

8. I tolerate no biased remarks about any group of people.

9. I seek peer support to counter frustration resulting from overt and covert acts of racism toward my children, my family, or me.

10. I seek support and guidance from others who have a personal understanding of racism, particularly those from my child's race or birth culture.

11. I have acquired practical information about how to deal with insensitive questions from strangers.

12. I help my children understand that being discriminated against does not reflect personal shortcomings.

13. I am able to validate my children's feelings, including anger and hurt related to racism or discrimination."

"It is good to have other cultures in your family.
In your heart you know you are making the world more open."
~10 year old African American adoptee, New Jersey

Racial Awareness - Near the end of her adoption journey, one mom suggested that since they were adopting their Chinese son into their Greek family, he "will simply have to learn to be Greek," since they had no intention of incorporating his Chinese culture into their lives. She ended with this statement. "What does that (his culture) have to do with us? He has a new life now." This shows a lack of sensitivity to her son's culture and a lack of awareness of her son's psychological, emotional, and cultural needs.

Racial Awareness refers to the adoptive parent's ability to examine their personal attitudes and understandings of how the dynamics of "race, culture, language, ethnicity, and power status" affect their lives and the lives of others as it relates to "racism, oppression, and other forms of discrimination."[69]

Once again, I refer to the work of Elizabeth Vonk. She provides twelve recommendations to help you develop racial awareness. They correlate to awareness of self- and other- awareness, as well as sensitivity to racism.

1. "I understand how my own cultural background influences the way I think, act, and speak.

2. I am able to recognize my own racial prejudice.

3. I am aware of stereotypes and preconceived notions that I may hold toward other racial and ethnic minority groups.

4. I have examined my feelings and attitudes about the birth culture and race of my children.

5. I make ongoing efforts to change my own prejudiced attitudes.

6. I have thoroughly examined my motivation for adopting a child of a different race or culture than myself.

7. I am knowledgeable of and continue to develop respect for the history and culture of my children's racial heritage.

8. I understand the unique needs of my child related to his or her racial or cultural status.

9. I know that transracial-cultural adoptive parenting involves extra responsibilities over and above those of in racial parenting.

10. I have examined my feelings about interracial dating and marriage.

11. I know that others may view my family as "different."

12. I know that my children may be treated unkindly or unfairly because of racism."

Caution Signs

Some parents have difficulty connecting with the traumatic and emotional losses our children bring with them. The experiences of our children are rooted in the repeated formation and traumatic disruption of relationships. These experiences will not simply disappear when we greet our children with waiting arms and bring them into our loving homes. Adoptive parents must know that repeated broken relationships, even at very early ages, inhibit a child's ability to trust and feel secure in their changing environments. Remember: *these kids do not know us.* They will learn about us only by how we demonstrate our love, concern, and care for every aspect of their lives, including their races and cultures.

My hope is to better prepare you to parent your fostered and adopted children with empathy, patience, understanding, respect, and cultural competence. Our children's culture is their birthright. When parents recognize this truth, finding ways to honor culture becomes a joyful exploration of who their children are. The result will be a strong and loving bond between parents and children. Parents well bonded to their children are parents who can influence with love, and heal even the deepest wounds.

Conclusion

In previous portions of this book we touched on some of the traumatic challenges children face when they come from foster care and move into adoption. Children adopted transracially add the loss of connection and relationship with their culture as well. If we are ready to accept children who are culturally or ethnically different from ourselves, must we also embrace their culture? Our only answer must be *yes*!

Parenting children of a race or culture not our own provides us with new possibilities for personal growth and expands the unlimited love and respect we impart in our relationships with our children. Our privileged responsibility is to reconnect our children with their heritage both past and present.

By deciding to honor and respect the rich ethnic cultures of our children, we instill within them a growing pride of who they are and how well they are loved. As one father tells me, "My heritage is who I am, and who I have become through the ages. My child deserves to know and grow in this same truth. I honor my child's heritage because honoring my own is so important to me."

You have come a long way on your journey. Your once distant dream of family now looms as a clear vision just over the next small rise in the road. Drive on with anticipation, dear parent. You are almost home.

Uncommon & Limitless Love Journal Activity

What will you do if a family member, friend, or neighbor cannot accept your decision and your new child? This would be a wonderful opportunity to further clarify your personal reasons for adopting across cultures. What do you foresee as the highest benefits? What obstacles loom before you, your child, and your family in this regard?

> As you are discovering throughout this journey journaling is a self-healing, self-actuating, and values illuminating activity.
>
> · Use it now to formulate positive responses to possible negative or indifferent reactions you or your child may receive from others.
>
> · Use it now to draw out and find solutions to your own internal conflicts about ethnicity, race, and culture.
>
> · Use it now to create a positive and resource rich plan for living a multicultural lifestyle and promoting racial awareness strength in your family circle.

By adopting transracially, you have unwittingly opened yourself to become an ambassador of diversity and unity among all peoples. You must develop the strength to be a model of acceptance and inclusion that reaches far beyond tolerance. Journal about how you intend to follow through with this mission. Life never ceases to surprise us!

Back Up & Restore

12 WAYS TO HONOR THE CULTURE, ETHNICITY, AND HERITAGE OF YOUR ADOPTED CHILD

Parenting with Global Awareness

Children adopted cross-culturally struggle to fill the gap between the culture and ethnicity of their adoptive parents and the development of their own ethnic and cultural identities. What can parents do to nurture and support healthy cultural identities in their adopted children? The following suggestions will help you become a global parent.

- Research to understand your child's racial, cultural, and ethnic origins internationally and domestically

- Have your family choose a new custom or tradition to practice and celebrate together

- Erase and replace lingering notions of stereotypes associated with persons of your child's race by visiting the child's country of origin, touring related historical properties, and getting accurate cultural information

- Get to know others who share the ethnicity and cultural history of your child

- Form friendships and alliances in the community, and ask them to mentor you, as you try to raise your child with awareness of his or her ethnic heritage

- Explore what cultural and ethnic events and holidays you can celebrate together

- Develop a genuine appreciation for your child's culture through education, experience, association, and life

- Visit museums, concerts, art shows, and other cultural events, which best portrays your child's culture
- Honor your child by bringing ethnic art, literature, music, food, and textiles into your home, and incorporating it proudly and prominently in family life
- Display photos of your child, photos of your child in cultural dress, photos of his or her birth family, or important cultural items he or she may have brought with them in places of honor
- Purchase books or magazines whose articles and images enrich your child's connections with who they are and provide strong moral character and ethnic pride
- Join a local foster or adoption support group with member families that mirror your own

Parenting a transracially adopted child requires us to examine with new awareness our pre-established social perspectives and former paradigms. Parenting with a global awareness allows us to open ourselves to the collective richness of all people, their culture, language, traditions, and ancient wisdom. Modeling acceptance through understanding, acknowledging our human kinship, appreciating the diverse beauty and hue of every face, will nurture a strong healthy identity in our adopted children.

CHAPTER TEN

HOME

You Have Arrived

"Oh, the comfort
– the inexpressible comfort of feeling safe with a person
– having neither to weigh thoughts or measure words,
but pouring them all right out, just as they are, chaff and grain together;
certain that a faithful hand will take and sift them, keep what is worth keeping,
and then with the breath of kindness blow the rest away."
~Dinah Craik, A Life For A Life, 1859

Today is Adoption Day! This is the day you waited for so long. Today, at least for a little while, *you have arrived.*

When do you *know* you have arrived?

Where is the milestone that marks the journey's end?

How do you measure the distance you have come, how you have changed, and all you have learned on the journey?

When you arrive at your destination, does the distance traveled matter any longer?

Do you forget the hardship of the trip in the joyful planning of a new journey about to begin? And, no matter what the emotional toll expended, does it all fade away when you look into the bright and lovely face of *your* child?

Today is Adoption Day!

For this day you,
- Attended every class required
- Participated in a bonding evaluation with your child
- Suffered through the uncertainty of the state's search for biological relatives *suitable to take your child.*

For this day you,
- Subjected yourselves willingly to state inspections of your home
- Openly shared the most intimate details of your life.

For the sake of this day,
- You waited long...
- Wondered if...
- Worried when...
- Trusting - you endured.

You did it all for the sake of this one, wonderful blessed day.

Adoption Day Journal Entry – April 24, 2003

We arrive at the courthouse in cars filled with family and friends. Dressed in our finest and laden with cameras we climb the granite steps to the courthouse and ride the elevator in shifts to the 2nd floor. We enter into a corridor filled with families. There are children and babies, mothers and fathers, aunts and uncles, grandparents, cousins and siblings. There are balloons and bows, little suits and ruffled dresses, smiles and laughter, new toys and fresh flowers. Though we are strangers, we are connected by our collective experience, connected by the fulfillment of our hopes and dreams on this day, and by the overflowing emotion of the moment.

Some sit on the wide windowsills, others stand in small intimate groups. Family names are called one by one and whole extended families leave the corridor and disappear behind closed doors. Now and then muffled laughter comes floating out into the hall, while we who are left exchange happy grins in anticipation of what is soon to come.

When our name is called we enter in to the courtroom. Along with our entourage of family and friends are our daughter's caseworker, and our two best family friends who will stand as our witnesses. The judge begins to speak but it is hard to focus on all that he is saying, until he says these words: "This child will be your child, having all the rights and inheritances of any child, as if born to you."

I hear the sniffles from the benches behind me and I see my husband wipe a tear from his face. I hold our 'new' daughter on my lap a little closer. I can smell her hair and feel her soft brown skin. She grasps my fingers. This is it. In just 15 minutes, with a few simple words, she is ours at last.

The gavel strikes loudly and applause and cheers erupt. My husband and the judge are shaking hands and comparing their ties from 'Save the Children.' Cameras are clicking to capture every moment. Our little daughter, 32 months old, explores the room hesitantly. The court secretary brings out a large, beautiful teddy bear and presents it to our daughter. It is bigger than she is. With that we are off. At home awaits 75 of our closest friends and family, food, music, and the mother-of-all-adoption parties. It is time to celebrate our family!

Conclusion

Yes, dear parent, you have arrived. This day, Adoption Day, is only a day of rest in your travels. Some call it a honeymoon between child and parent. After the party you will settle in as a family and slowly grow into knowing one another. Even though you may have been together for some time, this too constitutes change and transition to your child. Expect that it will be a process.

Know that your journey does not end here. There is so much growth and discovery, struggle and joy, yet to be had.

"Promise me you'll always remember.
You are braver than you believe,
and stronger than you seem, and smarter than you think."
~Christopher Robin to Pooh

Remember also, that you are never really alone. Countless thousands share stories like your own. Take all you have learned here to heart. Tuck it away safely with all your resources. Return to it should you ever need support.

For now, all is well. The journey may have been long, but you are a family now. As a family you have come home.

Back Up & Restore

TALKING TO CHILDREN ABOUT ADOPTION

"Many days and nights went by, but the problems did not go away. Again and again Mother Bird tried to weave new twigs and straw into the new nest, but it was not strong enough to hold the growing baby bird. She tried to bring enough food to him and keep him warm but he was soon hungry and crying again. Mother Bird was very sad. She understood that a baby bird, which did not have a safe nest and did not have enough food to eat was a baby bird in some danger. As she grew more and more tired, she began to think that even though she was doing everything she knew how to do, she wasn't taking good enough care of her baby."[70]

~Anne Braff Brodzinsky, PhD, *An Adoption Story, The Mulberry Bird*

Talking to your child about being adopted is admittedly an emotional subject for many adoptive parents. All experts and adoption specialists agree that children need to know they are adopted from the very beginning of their journey. But when or how do you tell them? What words do you use? How much do you say? How often should adoptive parents talk about adoption issues with their children? At what age will they really understand what it all means? These are some of the questions I am certain gnaw at your heart. Don't worry. Our children will have a few questions of their own, and they will be asking them soon enough. Take a deep breath, dear parents, and release all that stored up anxiety. Did you think the journey was over? It has only just begun.

My Personal Story

I sat on the sofa with my three-year-old daughter snuggled up next to me. We had just finished reading a Mr. Rogers book about adoption. She sat with the book in her lap looking at the pictures. I knew I couldn't let it go any longer without telling her.

She came to us as an infant. The differences between us were evident. "My skin is dark brown, Daddy has light brown, and Mommy's skin is pink," she would say. She had had weekly visitation with her birth mother for more than a year after she was born. We spoke openly about adoption in front of her all the time. She knew how she came to be with us. Yet, I knew she didn't know. Not really.

Several times I opened my mouth to speak. My eyes began to burn and I took a deep breath to push back my emotions. She turned the pages of the book and never looked at me, so it was easier to hide my well of tears. I thought to myself, "This is silly. Of course, I didn't give birth to her! I know that!" But my heart betrayed me. I had waited for her. I had longed for her long before she ever came. I had chosen her name before I had ever seen her face. Amid the turmoil of foster care, visitation, and relative searches, my emotions had run wild wondering if we would actually get to keep her with us. Fearful we would not.

Now she was going to be with us forever. But did she understand? I *felt* like she was mine all along, and suddenly I was sitting there searching deeply for the right words to tell her that she had had another mother. And, I didn't want to hurt her. I desperately didn't want to cause her more pain. I didn't want to completely strip away what security she now felt. I felt my heart swell, and I began to speak.

"I love you very much. Did you know I wasn't always your mother? You had another mother who gave birth to you. She loved you too, but she had many difficulties in her life and had to give you up...that's when we found you." I waited. I held my breath and my tears.

Her head stayed down and she stopped turning the pages. She looked up at me and asked. "Was it you? Were you the mommy who couldn't keep me, and now you have me back?" "Did you come and find me, Mommy?" I swallowed hard. I went on to tell her the same story I had spoken to so many others so many times before. We took her Life Book out to refresh her young memories.

Because of her age I kept most of the details out...those difficult details and other stories so hard to hear, and hard to speak to a child. Those can come later, when she is ready and older, when she begins to ask and wonder.

On the other hand, if she fails to ask - what then? I will always open the conversation. I will invite her to talk about it and ask her questions. I will be ready to give her answers in a way that she will know we are fine.

The conversation that day was short, a few sentences really. That was all she or I could do in the moment. Then we played a game of hide and seek.

Questions From The Other Side

The questions may be different. The details may change. The ages of the children will be any age and every age. What will you reply when your child asks you:

- "What's 'dopted mean?"

- "Why did you pick me?"

- "How did you ever get me from my *real* parents? I know they would NEVER let anybody have me."

- "What's wrong with me? Why didn't anybody else in my family want me?"

- "Did I ever have brothers and sisters in my other family?"
- "Mommy, if you ever don't love me anymore, will you give me away too?"
- "Will I ever see my foster parents and foster brother again?"
- "Where do you think my *real* mom is now? Can I ever go see her?"

These are real questions from real children to their adoptive parents. Soon, you will be *real* adoptive parents too. What will your answers be? Think about that...

Life *is* a roller coaster. The car may have stopped, but you've got kids now! You'd better have your running shoes on!

ABOUT AUTHOR

Deborah A. Beasley, ACPI CCPF, is a Coach for Parents and Families, parent educator, published author, presenter, and has served as a child advocate on several boards since 2007. She is a graduate of The Academy for Coaching Parents International in Texas, USA. Deborah holds six Certifications and is a member of the International Association of Coaches. She has over 15 published articles in online magazines. Deborah is also a Reiki Practitioner and utilizes her knowledge of body energy to teach clients effective self-regulation and stress relief. Deborah is the founder and Director of Together At Last Family Support, in Pitman, New Jersey, improving the parenting experience of adoptive and special needs parents through providing trauma based education, parent coaching services, and peer support groups through all the stages of parenting.

Deborah lives in southern New Jersey and is happily married to her husband of twenty-nine years. She is the mother of seven with ages ranging from 8 to 35, and grandmother of seven. She is a dedicated and loving mom, step-mom, adoptive mom, grand mom and former foster mom. She firmly believes that no child is expendable and neither are those that care for them. She is passionate about the work she does with and for her diverse clients.

Deborah's education began years before her acceptance into The Academy for Coaching Parents International (ACPI), when she began searching for answers to help her own trauma-affected children. Her mission led her to a seminar on *Reactive Attachment Disorder and Oppositional Defiant Disorder* given in Philadelphia, in 2007. It was through the introduction to current research on the connection between neuroscience, behavior, trauma, and relationship, that Deborah and her husband found renewed hope for their family.

In addition to her comprehensive training in child development through ACPI, Deborah has attended many trainings and seminars that focus on intense aspects of the traumatic effect of children's behaviors and mental health concerns. Deborah now has earned six educational certifications. Training titles include

Intensive Attachment and Somatic Body Experience

Advanced Mindfulness

Integrating Meditation and Cutting-Edge Neuroscience in the effective treatment of anxiety, depression, and anger.

Her blog features articles that address the many layers of special needs parenting today. Deborah provides professional coaching services by phone and in home for parents with adoptive, biological, and special needs parenting concerns. She and her colleagues at Together At Last Family Support also offer family coaching and consultation services and a variety of workshop and training opportunities.

Contact Deborah to arrange Parenting and Trauma trainings at your location and for coaching and family or behavioral consultation services at: 609-970-1100. Visit Together At Last Family Support on the web at:

www.TogetherAtLastFamily.com

RESOURCES

Books

Affect Regulation and the Development of Psychopathology, Susan Bradley, The Guilford Press, © 2003

Helping Kids Cope with Stress and Trauma, Nurturing Peace and Balance, Caron Goode, Ed.D. Tom Goode, N.D., and David Russell SFO M.F.A. Ph.D., Inspired Living International, LLC, © 2006

Trauma Through A Child's Eyes, Awakening the Ordinary Miracle of Healing, Infancy through Adolescence, Peter A. Levine, Ph.D. and Maggie Kline, MS, MFT, ERGOS Institute Press, © 2007

Waking the Tiger, Healing Trauma, The Innate Capacity to Transform Overwhelming Experiences, Peter A. Levine, Ph.D., and Ann Frederick, North Atlantic Books, © 1997

Touchpoints, The Essential Reference, Your Child's Emotional and Behavioral Development, T. Berry Brazelton, M.D., Addison-Wesley Publishing Co., © 1992

What's Best for Kids, A Guide to Developmentally Appropriate Practices for Teachers and Parents of Children Age 4-8, Anthony Coletta, Ph.D., Modern Learning Press, © 1991

The Discipline Book, How to Have a Better-Behaved Child from Birth to Age Ten, William Sears, M.D., and Martha Sears, R.N., Little, Brown and Company, © 1995

The Explosive Child, A New Approach for Understanding and Parenting Easily Frustrated, Chronically Inflexible Children, Ross Greene, Ph.D., Harper Press, © 2005

The Biology of Belief – Unleashing the Power of Consciousness, Matter, and Miracles, Bruce H. Lipton, Ph.D., Hay House, Inc., © 2011

Mindful Therapy A Guide for Therapists and Helping Professionals, Thomas Bien, Ph.D., Wisdom Publications, Inc., © 2006

Giving the Love That Heals, A Guide for Parents, Harville Hendrix, Ph.D., and Helen Hunt, M.A., M.L.A., Pocket Books, A Division of Simon and Schuster, © 1997

Connection Parenting, Parenting through Connection instead of Coercion, Through Love instead of Fear, Pam Leo Wyatt-MacKenzie Publishing, Inc., © 2005, 2007

Beyond Consequences, Logic, and Control, A Love Based Approach to Helping Children with Severe Behaviors, Heather T. Forbes, LCSW and B. Bryan Post, LCSW, Vol. 1 and 2, Beyond Consequences Institute, © 2007, 2009, 2010

The Attachment Parenting Book – A Common sense Guide to Understanding and Nurturing Your Baby, William Sears and Martha Sears, Little Brown, © 2001

Nurture Your Child's Gift, Inspired Parenting, Caron B. Goode, Ed.D., Atria Books, A Division of Simon and Schuster, © 2001, 2008

Being Adopted, The Lifelong Search for Self, David M. Brodzinsky, Ph.D., Marshall D. Schechter, M.D., and Robin Marantz Henig, Anchor Books, A Division of Random House, Inc., © 1993, 1992

Twenty Things Adopted Kids Wish Their Adoptive Parents Knew, Sherrie Eldridge, Dell Publishing, A Division of Random House, © 1999

The Family of Adoption, Joyce Maguire Pavao, Beacon Press, © 1998

The Seven Habits of Highly Effective People, Powerful Lessons in Personal Change, Seven R. Covey, Published by Simon and Schuster, © 1989, Fireside Books, © 1990

Research and Published Papers

Cultural Socialization in Families With Internationally Adopted Children, Richard M. Lee, Harold D. Grotevant, Wendy L. Hellerstedt, Megan R. Gunnar, and The Minnesota International Adoption Project Team, University of Minnesota, Twin Cities Campus Journal of Family Psychology Copyright 2006 by the American Psychological Association 2006, Vol. 20, No. 4, 571–580 0893-3200/06 DOI: 10.1037/0893-3200.20.4.571 Used with permission.

The Transracial Adoption Paradox: History, Research, and Counseling "Implications of Cultural Socialization" Richard M. Lee, University of Minnesota Published in: The Counseling Psychologist vol.31 No. 6 Nov. 2003 711-744 DOI: 10.1177/0011000003258087 (c) 2003 by the Division of Counseling Psychology. Used with permission.

Cultural Competence for Transracial Adoptive Parents, M. Elizabeth Vonk, PhD., LISW, University of Ohio, © 2001, Social work by National Association of Social Workers in the format other book via Copyright Clearance Center. Order Detail ID: 58688302 Used with permission.

DVD's and MP3 Recordings and Teleseminar Conferences

Linda Curran's Trauma Competency Stabilization, with Linda A. Curran, BCPC, LPC, CACD, CCDP-D, PESI, Inc. Along with: *Trauma Competency A Clinician's Guide*

Trauma, Brain and Relationship, Helping Children Heal –From Neurons to Neighborhoods Community Conferences, Sponsored by Santa Barbara Graduate Institute Center for Clinical Studies and Research

How to Learn from the Unspoken Voice of Trauma - A Teleseminar Session with Peter Levine, PhD, and Ruth Buczynski, PhD, The National Institute for the Clinic al Application of Behavioral Medicine, © 2011 www.nicabm.com

A Hands-on Approach to Treating Trauma and Building Resilience - A Teleseminar Session with Glenn Schiraldi, PhD and Ruth Buczynski, Ph.D., The National Institute for the Clinical Application of Behavioral Medicine, © 2011 www.nicabm.com

The Polyvagal Theory for Treating Trauma - A Teleseminar Session with Stephen W. Porges, PhD and Ruth Buczynski, PhD, The National Institute for the Clinical Application of Behavioral Medicine, © 2011 www.nicabm.com

Affect Regulation and Mind-Brain-Body Healing of Trauma - A Teleseminar Session with Allan N. Schore, PhD and Ruth Buczynski, PhD, The National Institute for the Clinical Application of Behavioral Medicine, © 2011 www.nicabm.com

ENDNOTES

1 The Evan B. Donaldson Institute,
www.adoptioninstitute.org/FactOverview/foster

2 Ibid.

Chapter One

3 Dictionary.com http://dictionary.reference.com/browse/attunement

Chapter Two

4 www.kidlaw.com – Child Placement Review Board Proceedings - PDF

5 Office of Public Defender, New Jersey , 2007
www.state.nj.us/defecder/div_lawguardian

6 Ibid.

Chapter Three

7 www.ndaa.org/pdf/ncpca_statute_child_neglect_abandonment_3_07.pdf

8 Child Welfare Information Gateway, A Service of the Children's Bureau,
Administration for Children and Families, U.S. Department of Health and
Human Service www.hhs.gov

9 Ibid.

10 The Center for Disease Control, www.cdc.gov/ViolencePrevention/child-
maltreatment/index

11 Child Welfare Information Gateway, A Service of the Children's Bureau,
Administration for Children and Families, U.S. Department of Health and
Human Service www.hhs.gov

12 Ibid.

13 Ibid.

14 Ibid.

15 NASW Standards for Cultural Competence in Social Work Practice, copyright 2001 by National Association of Social Workers. Reproduced with
permission of National Association of Social Workers in the format Other
book via Copyright Clearance Center.
www.socialworkers.org/practice/standars/NASWCulturalStandards.pdf

16 Child Welfare Information Gateway, A Service of the Children's Bureau,
Administration for Children and Families, U.S. Department of Health and
Human Service www.hhs.gov

17 Urban Institute Child Welfare Research Program Foster Care Adoption in the United States A state by state Analysis of Barriers and Promising Approaches (Introduction) - Jennifer Ehrle Macomber, Cynthia Andrews Scarcella, Erica H. Zielewski, Rob Geen, http://www.urban.org/url.cfm?ID=411108

This report was commissioned by The National Adoption Day Coalition. The National Adoption Day Coalition, comprised of seven partners—The Alliance for Children's Rights, Casey Family Services, Children's Action Network, Congressional Coalition on Adoption Institute, Dave Thomas Foundation for Adoption®, Freddie Mac Foundation and Target Corporation—commissioned the authors to conduct this state-by-state analysis to identify the common barriers and promising approaches that exit in the process of adopting children from the foster care system across the country.

The nonpartisan Urban Institute publishes studies, reports, and books on timely topics worthy of public consideration. The views expressed are those of the authors and should not be attributed to the Urban Institute, its trustees, or its funders.

18 Ibid. Stages to Adoption, page 3 and Glossary and Key Acronyms, pages 14 and 15.

19 Ibid. Key Findings: Barriers to Foster Care Adoption page 7.

Chapter Five

20 The 7 Habits of Highly Effective People Powerful Lessons in Personal Change, by Steven R. Covey, Simon and Schuster, 1989 Habit 4, Principles of Interpersonal Leadership, pages 220 – 222.

21 Urban Institute Child Welfare Research Program, Foster Care Adoption in the United States A state by state Analysis of Barriers and Promising Approaches, pages 18 through 122.

22 Child Welfare Information Gateway – A service of the Children's Bureau, Administration of Children and Families, U.S. Department of Health and Human Services, Reform Based on Litigation – Information Packet: Child Welfare Class Action Lawsuits, Kaplan, May 2003.

23 PDF – National Resource Center for Foster Care and Permanency Planning at the Hunter College School of Social Work, Child Welfare Class Action Lawsuits, by Rhonda Kaplan, May 2003, pages 6, 7, and 8.

24 Ibid.

25 2001, revised 2004 Gary Baran & CNVC. The right to freely duplicate this document is hereby granted.

26 Kith and Kin – One's acquaintances and relatives. The American Heritage Dictionary of the English Language Fourth Edition, 2000, by Houghton Mifflin Company. All rights reserved.

27 Karoline Meyer:
http://video.google.com/videoplay?docid=6965212229879236740#

28 Mindful Therapy A Guide for Therapists and Helping Professionals –
Thomas Bien, Chapter 3 – Mindfulness is the Key, page 58 – 59, 2006,
Wisdom Publications.

29 PDF – American Psychological Association, Stress in America Findings
Report, November 2010.

30 Transcendental Meditation – TM refers to the Transcendental Meditation
technique, a specific form of mantra meditation, and to the Transcendental Meditation movement, a spiritual movement. The TM technique
and TM movement were introduced in India in the mid- 1950s by Mahar-
ishi Mahesh Yogi (1914 – 2008) and had reached global proportions by
the 1960s. http://en.widipedia.org/wiki/Transcendental_Meditation

31 NCCAM – National Institutes of Health – The National Center for Complementary and Alternative Medicine, What is Complementary and
Alternative Medicine? Types of CAM
www.nccam.nih.gov/health/whatiscam/

32 Wikipedia: Gautama Buddha –
http://en.wikipedia.org/wiki/Gautama_Buddha

33 Mindful Therapy A Guide for Therapists and Helping Professionals, by
Thomas Bien, Ph.D., The Noble Eightfold Path, pages 168 – 188, 2006,
Wisdom Publications

34 King James Bible (KJV), Matthew Chapter 5, verses 1 – 12. Published by
Zondervan, 1994.

35 From the Blog: Quotes.Posterous.com

Chapter Six

36 Native American Wisdom at www.crazybear.org

37 Child/Teen Attachment Therapy Corrective Attachment Parenting, By
Terry Levy, Ph.D., and Michael Orleans, M.A., Evergreen Psychotherapy
Center Attachment Treatment and Training Institute, Evergreen, CO
www.attachmentexperts.com/childteen

38 National Resource Center for Family-Centered Practice and Permanency
Planning, Foster Parent Pre-Service Training, (Individual state require-
ments for foster parent training in the U.S.) Hunter College of Social
Work, 2008

39 Affect Regulation and Mind, Brain, Body Healing of Trauma, Alan Shore,
2011, from the National Institute for the Clinical Application of Behavioral
Medicine

40 U.S. Public Health Service, Report of the Surgeon General's Conference
on Children's Mental Health: A National Action Agenda, Washington, DC:
Department of Health and Human Services, 2000.

41 Mental Illness in Children, 2009, WebMD, LLC.

42 Affect Regulation and the Development of Psychopathology, Susan J. Bradley, Chapter 5, Stress, Trauma, and Abuse, page 91, 2000, The Guilford Press

43 Trauma Through A Child's Eyes, Awakening the Ordinary Miracle of Healing, Infancy Through Adolescence, Peter A. Levine, Maggie Kline Chapter 2, pages 21 – 33.

44 Report of the Surgeon General's Conference on Children's Mental Health: A National Action Agenda, Washington, DC, 2000, Stock No. 017-024-01659-4
ISBN No. 0-16-050637-9 -
http://www.surgeongeneral.gov/topics/cmh/childreport.html

45 "When a Parents 'I love you' Means 'Do as I Say'", by Alfie Kohn, The New York Times, 2009.

46 Beyond Consequences, Logic, and Control, A Love Based Approach to Helping Children With Severe Behaviors, Heather T. Forbes, LCSW and B. Bryan Post, LCSW Chapter One, The Stress Model Principles of a New Understanding, page 5, Beyond Consequences Institute, 2009.

47 Trauma, Brain, and Relationship Helping Children Heal, DVD, Sponsored by the Santa Barbara Graduate Institute Center for Clinical Studies an Research, 2004

48 The Biology of Belief: Unleashing the Power of Consciousness, Matter, and Miracles, by Bruce Lipton, 2005

49 Perry, BD, Incubated in Terror: Neurodevelopmental Factors in the 'Cycle of Violence' In: Children, Youth, and Violence, The Search for Solutions (J Olsofsky, Ed. Guilford Press, New York, pp 124 – 148, 1997, online at www.childtrauma.org (Child Trauma Academy Materials) page 12

50 Beyond Consequences, Logic and Control, A Love-Based Approach to Helping Children with Severe Behaviors, Heather T. Forbes, LCSW, and B. Bryan Post, LCSW, Chapter One The Stress Model, page 7, Beyond Consequences Institute, 2009

51 The Effects of Early Relational Trauma on Right Brain Development, Affect Regulation, and Infant Mental Health, Allen Shore, 2001, Published in Infant Journal of Mental Health, pages 22, and 201 – 269.

52 Trauma Through a Child's Eyes Awakening the Ordinary Miracle of Healing, Infancy Through Adolescence, Peter A. Levine, Maggie Kline, Chapter 1, pages 4 – 5.

53 New York School of Medicine, Child Study Center Letter, The Aftermath of Disaster: Helping Children Affected by Trauma and Death, 2002, vol. 1 no. 1

54 Ibid.

55 Developmental Trauma Disorder: Towards a Rational Diagnosis of Children with Complex Trauma Histories, Bessel A. Van der Kolk, M.D.

56 'The Effects of Trauma on Children and the Role of Mental Health Services', Charles G. Curie, M.A., A.C.S.W., U.S. Department of Health and Human Services before the Senate Committee of Health, Education, Labor and Pensions, 2002

57 'Developmental Trauma Disorder: Towards a Rational Diagnosis of Children with Complex Trauma Histories', Bessel A. Van der Kolk, M.D., The Dynamics of Childhood Trauma, pages 6 – 7.

58 Ibid. Trauma, Caregivers, and Affect Tolerance, pages 4 – 5.

59 'An Evaluation of Adjustment Based Upon the Concept of Security,' Mary Salter (later Ainsworth), 1940, page 45.

Chapter Nine

60 The Evan B Donaldson Adoption Institute, www.adoption institute.org/research/adoptionfacts

61 'The Transracial Adoption Paradox: History, Research and Counseling Implications of Cultural Socialization', Richard M. Lee, University of Minnesota, The Counseling Psychologist, Vol. 31 No.6, November 2003, 711-744, DOI: 10.1177/0011000003258087, by the division of Counseling Psychology. Used with Permission.

62 Ibid. Transracial Adoption, page 714.

63 'Cultural Socialization in Families with International Adopted Children,' Richard M. Lee, Harold D. Grotevant, Wendy L. Hellerstedt, Megan R. Gunnar, and the Minnesota International Adoption Project Team, University of Minnesota, Twin Cities Campus, Journal of Family Psychology, 2006, by the American Psychological Association, Vol. 20 No. 4, 571-580 0893-3200/06 DOI: 10.1037/0893-3200.20.4.571 Used with Permission.

64 Ibid. DeBerry, et al (1996) and Yoon (2001), page 720. A study of African American and Korean adolescent adoptees in the United States.

65 Used with permission of M. Elizabeth Vonk, PhD., LISW, University of Ohio, Cultural Competence for Transracial Adoptive Parents, 2001, Social work by National Association of Social Workers in the format of Other book, via Copyright Clearance Center. Order Detail ID: 58688302.

66 Ibid. Multicultural Planning. Reproduced and used with permission as above.

67 Used with permission of M. Elizabeth Vonk, PhD., LISW, University of Ohio, Cultural Competence for Transracial Adoptive Parents, 2001, Social work by National Association of Social Workers in the format of Other book, via Copyright Clearance Center, Order Detail ID: 58788302.

68 Ibid. Survival Skills. Reproduced and used with permission as above.

69 Ibid. Racial Awareness. Reproduced and used with permission as above.

Chapter Ten

70 An Adoption Story The Mulberry Bird, Anne Braff Brodzinsky, PhD., 1996, Perspectives Press. "All rights reserved... except in the case of brief quotations embodied in critical articles and reviews."